EXCELLING
as a TEAM LEADER

Helping Team Members & the Unit Be Best in Field

FORTIUS (stronger) CITIUS (faster) ALTIUS (higher)

This manual introduces The Triangle Team Leadership Model which contains a mission statement that unites members of a department, division and organization and has three connecting programs that managers can use to help direct reports be best in their field advancing their career while helping the team unit be best in its functional area and the organization be best in its industry.

Michael V. Mulligan Ph.D.
Executive Career and Business Coach

EXCELLING AS A TEAM LEADER
HELPING TEAM MEMBERS & THE UNIT BE BEST IN FIELD

iUniverse books may be ordered through booksellers or by contacting:

iUniverse
1663 Liberty Drive
Bloomington, IN 47403
www.iuniverse.com
1-800-Authors (1-800-288-4677)

Because of the dynamic nature of the Internet, any web addresses or links contained in this book may have changed since publication and may no longer be valid. The views expressed in this work are solely those of the author and do not necessarily reflect the views of the publisher, and the publisher hereby disclaims any responsibility for them.

Any people depicted in stock imagery provided by Getty Images are models, and such images are being used for illustrative purposes only.
Certain stock imagery © Getty Images.

ISBN: 978-1-5320-4168-6 (sc)
ISBN: 978-1-5320-4169-3 (e)

Print information available on the last page.

iUniverse rev. date: 02/24/2018

Table of Contents

A Meaningful Quote

"Success comes to those

Who become success conscious.

Failure comes to those

Who indifferently allow themselves to

Become failure conscious"

Napoleon Hill

Comments from the Author

Gallup[i] conducted research on leadership and said that 82% of the managers companies hire are bad choices. Is it that they are bad choices or is it that these managers are not properly trained or have a system in place to be an effective team leader? I have personally worked with over 2,000 individuals who were dismissed from their company and when I asked them to list the number one reason for their separation, over 90% said it had to do with the communication and working relationship between them and their boss. A team leader can bring out the best in their direct reports or kill their spirit driving them out the door. Can training and a career mentoring and performance management system make a difference?

It has been said over and over if the team players between two competitors are fairly equal, it is the coaching that will make the difference. I played on six championship teams in high school and college and the reason we were successful is that we had outstanding head coaches who put in a system that built team play and made us the best at our positions so we could beat our competition and be recognized as best in our field/league.

The Triangle Team Leadership Model is a process that managers can implement to help direct reports become the best or leaders in their work field. The *Model* contains the mission statement, *Being Best in Our Field*, that will unite all members of a team unit, division and organization plus three connecting programs that will help team leaders transform each of their reports into a career planner and an expert performer at their position so specific objectives are met making team members the best at their positions, the team unit best in its functional area and organization best in its industry.

The Model was developed to help executives, managers and supervisors excel as a team unit leader in their functional area and industry. If you ask why a department, division and an organization is successful, it is the team unit leader working with and through his/her direct reports to achieve predetermined objectives that makes it happen. If you ask why individuals reach their potential, are happy at work, perform at high levels, advance in their career and remain with their company, it has to do with how well team unit leaders lead, manage, mentor and bring out the best in their direct reports. This workbook contains *four sections*.

In **_section one_**, the _Triangle Team leadership Model_ reviews a planning process that focuses on developing a vision and mission statement and sample _Best in Our Field_ goals and objectives that need to be met so team members are best in their field, the team unit best in its functional area and organization best in its industry.

In **_section two_**, we offer the _Team Leader Analysis and Improvement Program._ You will review what the professionals say about leadership and managing and then have the opportunity to fill out self scoring assessments to learn more about yourself as a team leader and manager. You can then develop an improvement plan that will help you excel in your present and future management positions.

In **_section three_**, we will discuss the _TEAM Program._ This program evaluates your capability to direct team meetings and helps you analyze the group dynamics of the team. Most importantly, it builds a sharing and team play culture bringing team members together to develop and meet individual and team unit _Best in Our Field_ objectives.

In **_section four_**, you will learn the _One-On-One Career Mentoring and Performance Facilitation Program_, the key to advancing careers and the organization. We will describe the role of a _Career Mentor and_ assess your career knowledge and helping and performance facilitation skills so you can execute an improvement program so you will excel as a team unit leader.

Most importantly, we will focus on you using the _Task Expert Process_ to transform your direct reports into an expert at performing identified tasks so they meet the objectives that make them best at their position, the unit best in its functional area and the organization best in its industry. Once classified an expert performer in their present position, they can then target their next position and develop and execute a career preparation plan.

The One-On-One meeting is also vital in helping the team leader keep all members in line so the team works well together. The team leader can also give each team member the attention they desire and need as well as use the process as a performance evaluation system.

Section One

The Triangle Team Leadership Model

You will learn about the parts of the Model by completing the following three tasks.

Task # One

A Planning Process- Start with a Vision and Mission Statement for the Organization

(The Planning Process)

Setting a Vision for the Organization

- Identifies where the organization is today and whered we want the organization to be tomorrow.
- Reflects the organization's intent

Setting a Motivating Mission Statement

- *What we are in business to accomplish*
- *Provides guideline about our purpose*

Create Connecting Organization Structure

- *The organization needs to have a connecting organization structure to carry out the vision and mission of the company.*

Strategic Goals

- *Non measurable statements that provides direction to where organization wants to go*
- *Stated in broad terms to achieve mission and vision*

Objectives

- Action statements that are measurable. They have a starting point and ending point. Example includes: We will increase sales from 50 million to $75 million from January 1 to December 31, 20____.

Tasks

- Identify the tasks that you complete to meet objectives
- Use *Task Expert Process* to turn employees into an expert performer at their position so objectives are met.

Behaviors

- The way employees work together in meeting objectives and tasks.

Developing a Vision for the Organization

Where are we today?

What services or products do we offer today?

Who are our customers? Who buys our services and products?

Who is our competition and who controls the market? What does our competition offer that we do not?

Where do we want to be tomorrow?

What services and products should we offer tomorrow to make money?

What is our vision for the organization?

How should we brand and market our organization?

Establishing a Mission Statement

Leaders of organizations or team units need to develop a Mission Statement that will excite, motivate, unify and reward all employees in the company.

The *Triangle Team Leadership Model* recommends that CEOs and their Team Unit Leaders create a mission statement that will motivate and challenge their people to become expert performers or the "Best in their Field" so they can help their unit be the best in its functional area and the organization be the best in its industry The spotlight would be on applauding team unit members for completing their assigned tasks and meeting specific objectives.

The motivator is **challenge and being given attention**. The **mission** is being the *Best in Our Feld* so all employees can advance their career and the company makes profit. Below is Frederick Herzberg's Motivational Model

What Satisfies Employees	**What Motivates Employees**
Fair company policies and procedures	Challenge
Effective supervision	Achievement
Positive relationships with supervisors	Recognition
Excellent working conditions	Responsibility
Competitive salaries	Advancement
Productive relationships with peers	Growth
Balance between personal life and work	Additional Compensation
Excellent relationships with direct reports	
Status	
Security	

Please note in his *Model* that challenge, recognition, achievement, responsibility, advancement, growth and additional compensation all motivate employees and fit into the mission of *Being the Best in Our Field.*

If the leadership of an organization doesn't establish a mission statement, and growth objectives that will rally everyone together to give 100% effort, the company will never be the best. The company will continue to operate behind its competition and work will seem like drudgery to the workers.

Because there is so much diversity and lack of loyalty in the workplace today, it is crucial that a company create a mission that will excite, reward and unify everyone. Anytime you have a mission that each person believes in, you will see people banding together to work hard for that mission. The American Revolution, World War I and World War II were fought in the name of freedom. Everyone believed in the mission and many gave their lives for it.

The mission of **Being Best in Our Field** can be observed each fall as hundreds of college teams join in the pursuit of a national football championship. Everyone associated with the college becomes emotionally involved with the team as it strives to be ranked #1. As the season progresses and the team continues to win advancing in the ranks, the enthusiasm and excitement grows. At the end of the season, the four teams ranked the highest by the *College Football Ranking Committee* will play against one another for the national championship. To be a national champion is quite an honor and will help each college recruit the best high school players in the nation to keep them ranked at the top.

Being a championship organization can be an extremely moving experience. For a period of time, you can call yourself the best of the best. Have you ever played or been part of a championship team? How did you feel about it at that time and afterwards? Was it an experience you will always remember?.

The mission of being the best is illustrated in Maslow and Herzberg's work.

Maslow's Self Actualization Theory

Self
Actualization
"Being the Best"
Self Esteem
"Becoming the Best"
Social
"A Feeling of Belong"
Security
"Knowing You Have a Job
and Can Make Mistakes"
Survival
"Knowing You Can Eat and Pay the Bills"

Task # Two-

**Planning-Creating an Organization Structure-
The Triangle Team Leadership Model**

Dr. Mulligan likes what Dr. John Kotter (Harvard Professor) had to say about leadership and management and created the *Triangle Team Leadership Model* taking into account his four main points.

- The organizations senior team unit leaders should establish a vision and mission statement and growth objectives that take into account the legitimate interest of all stakeholders.
- Strategies and a plan should be established to help achieve the vision and mission and growth objectives and take into account organization forces and impediments.
- A strong performance partnership network system should be established to implement the business plan and strategies to achieve the objectives.
- Recruit and select a highly motivated group of influential key team unit leaders into the performance partnership network who are committed to making the vision and mission a reality and who want badly to achieve the Best in Our Field objectives.

*There are two phases that should be implemented to
meet the mission-Being Best in Our Field*

(Phase One) –
The Company needs to establish a *Performance Management and Evaluation Committee* to teach the *Model* and then coordinate and measure the progress of team units and individuals so the ratings are meaningful.

The evaluation team must be seen as non partial and this will give the program credibility. Scores would be reported monthly on team units and individuals and four quarterly assessments would be completed to determine where team units and individuals are at that time and what they have to do to be successful by the end of the year or designated time line. This committee or group would present the results and awards at the end at a special lunch or dinner.

It should be noted that when much attention is paid to individuals, performance will increase. Any one that has played sports knows that they play harder when hundreds are watching and cheering for them rather than just a few.

(Phase Two)

The organization, depending on its size, needs to learn how *The Triangle Team Leadership Model* can be established to connect employees working at Corporate headquarters, the divisions and the departments together.

A large company could call it the *Triple Triangle Team leadership Model.* A small or medium size company that has no divisions could call the process the Double Triangle Team Leadership Model (Company and Departments).

The **first triangle in the Triple Triangle Team Leadership Models** would include the CEO, the corporation (stakeholders) and Presidents of the Divisions. The CEO and Division Presidents would develop a vision and mission statement, Best In Our Field objectives, a business plan with strategies and a budget for the corporation. This group then selects and works with the team unit leaders (department heads) both at the corporate office and the divisions. The CEO and Division Presidents develop the *Corporate Best in Field* growth goals and objectives. The Division Presidents then work with their department heads to develop their own *Best in Field* objectives that tie into helping the Corporation and their Division be successful.

#1.The Corporate Triangle Team Leadership Model

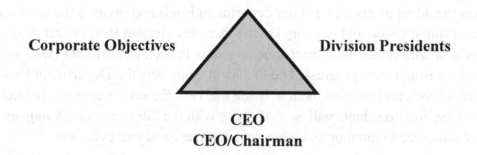

Corporate Objectives   **Division Presidents**

CEO
CEO/Chairman

The CEO meets with the Division Presidents to set the Corporate Objectives and Vision and Mission statements. The Board monitors and measures the results of the CEO. The CEO will meet monthly One-On-One with Division Presidents and will work closely with *The Performance Management & Evaluation Committee.* This group will coordinate, monitor and measure the results of the company, divisions, departments and individuals. The CEO and Division Presidents and Department Heads can go on line to see how every team unit is doing. Individuals who are not team unit leaders can go on line to learn how they are doing as an individual as well as their team unit. Individual reports should only be reviewed by the individual and his/her boss.

#2. *The Division Triangle Team Leadership Model*

The **second triangle** includes the Division President, the Division and Department Heads. The Division President reveals the corporate vision and mission statements, growth objectives and business plan. The President and Department Heads discuss the corporate vision, mission, growth objectives and business plan as it relates to their division. This Division partnership then develops their own vision and mission statements, growth objectives, business plan and strategies, budget and monitoring and measuring process to make their Division a Best in Field organization. The President and Department Heads develop their own Best in Field objectives that they have to meet to help their unit and the Division be successful and have themselves be rated an expert leader or performer.

The Division Triangle Team Leadership Model

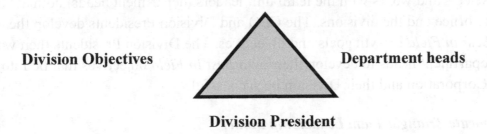

Division Objectives   **Department heads**

Division President

The Division President meets with his/her department heads and reviews the corporate objectives and stated vision and mission. He/she then sets division Best in Our field objectives with them.. He/she then meets one on one with each Department Head and monitors and measures their progress. The President empowers the Department Heads and counsels, advises and coaches them in using the Task Expert Process with direct reports. The Division Presidents will work directly with the *Performance Management & Evaluation Committee* to monitor and manage the process and rate everyone.

#3 *Department Triangle Team Leadership Model*

The **third triangle** includes a Department Head, the department itself, and direct reports. The Department Head shares with his/her direct reports the vision and mission statements, growth objectives, business plan and strategies and budget of the Division and Corporation. The department members then develop their own vision and mission statements, Best in Field objectives, business plan and strategies that need to be achieved to help the Corporation and Division achieve their objectives. The department needs to meet its established Best in Feld objectives to be rated the best in its' functional area.

The Department Triangle Team Leadership Model

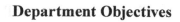 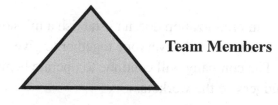

Department Objectives

Team Members

Department Head

The Department Head meets with team members to review the Corporate and Division Best in Field objectives. He/she then works with the team members to set the Best in Filed objectives of the department. The Department Head meets with reports monthly one on one to monitor and measure their progress using The *Task Expert Process*. The Department Head asks each team member to establish their own Best in Field or growth objectives and connect them to helping the department, division and corporation meet their objectives. The Department Head should counsel, advise and coach each team member so they meet their stated objectives and are ranked a task expert leader in their field.

The key to achieving the corporate and division business objectives depends on the departments meeting their objectives. John Kotter made the point clear that if senior team leaders are to be successful, they must develop a network of team unit leaders who will implement strategies beneficial to all stakeholders. There should be team unit leaders throughout the organization who are committed and prepared to execute the Triangle Team Leader Model.

Many CEOs seem convinced that their communication carries the biggest weight in the organization when it comes to impacting employees. A study of 164 CEOs in Fortune 500 companies by A. Forster Higgins & Company [xii] revealed that 95% of them believe their communication influenced employee job performance. The study reported that there was no evidence that communication from CEOs in large companies significantly affects employee behavior. A CEO can make a positive impression by being visible and walking around the company, but this behavior does not make an impact on each employee as much as a CEO might think. In most companies, it is too difficult for top leaders to know every employee well, so they need to rely on a properly situated, effective management team to do the communicating.

There is a wealth of supporting evidence to show that increasing the position power of managers and frontline supervisors influences employees more and builds organization cohesiveness. In the book *Communicating Change,* T.J. and Sandra Larkin [xiii] revealed several research studies showing the importance of empowering managers and supervisors.

The more position power a manager or supervisor is perceived to have, the more frontline employees will want to meet and work with that team leader.

If the leadership of an organization doesn't establish a mission statement, and champion building objectives that will rally everyone together to give 100% effort, the company will never be the best. The company will continue to operate behind its competition and work will seem like drudgery to the workers.

Task # Three-

Establish Best in Our Field Goals and Objectives for Organization

Before identifying goals and writing objectives, let's discuss the subject of goals and objectives. A goal provides direction and an objective is a specific description of an end result to be achieved. AN EFFECTIVE OBJECTIVE *SHOULD:*

1) be conceivable, believable and achievable
2) be measurable (numbers and times)
3) have a starting and ending time line
4) keep you focused on what and when you must do something
5) contain clear lines of responsibility and authority
6) be flexible so it can be changed at a given moment
7) be clearly understood
8) truly make your organization stand above the competition

The benefits of written objectives are:

* We avoid lapses in memory.
* There are fewer misunderstandings.
* They keep everyone on track: activities should be related to an end result.
* We can be adequately evaluated on results rather than activities.

Examples Objectives

Poor: Increase sales as much as we can under the circumstances.
Good: Increase the U.S. sales income in our sports helmet business from $500,000 to $600,000 for a net gain of $100,000 in 201_____.

Poor: Increase market share to where we can stay in business.
Good: Increase the U.S. market share in our sports helmet business from 45% to 50% in 201_____.

Implement the *GAP Analysis & Closure Model and Task Expert Process* to meet each reports, the unit and organization objectives: *The GAP Analysis & Closure Model* was developed to help you determine where you are, where you want to go and what tasks or activities you must do to close the gap. *The Task Expert Process* will help you work with reports to identify and complete the tasks necessary to meet the objectives and close the *Gap.*

11

Suggested Company and Unit (Division & Department) Goals and Objectives

We will provide sample *Being Best in Our Field* goals and objectives. The purpose of this exercise is to provide an opportunity for your company, division and department to identify goals and objectives that might be incorporated in the total *Best in Field* objectives package. If corporate does not use some of the suggested goals and objectives below and you think they are important, incorporate them into your division or department *Best in Field* goals and objectives. Your next challenge would be to identify and execute the tasks that direct reports need to complete to meet the predetermined objectives.

Goal One - Increase Your Income and Cash Flow

The corporate objectives could include:

1) Increase total sales income from _____ to _____ for the period beginning January 1 and ending December 31, 20_____.
2) Increase market share in each product/service by _____% for the period beginning January 1 and ending December 31, 20_____.
3) Select products/services with the most profit margin and increase sales in each by _____% in the year 20_____.
4) Increase our total customer base from _____ to _____ for the period beginning January 1 and ending December 31, 20_____.
5) Increase the expert performance of every employee and publish a company-wide expert book listing the experts in the organization so you save $_____ in consulting fees and $_____ in loss of employees because they never receive any recognition.
6) Increase net profit by _____% in 20_____..

Goal Two- Control and Manage Expenses So They Don't Exceed Your Income.

1) Develop a budget and aim to reduce it from_____ to _____ in 20_____.
2) Reduce benefit costs from_____ to _____% in 20_____.
3) Reduce the cost to produce each product by _____% or to deliver a service by _____% in 20_____.
4) Reduce absenteeism from _____to _____days.
5) Cut yearly costs from temporary employment services from _____ to _____ in 20_____.
6) Increase retention of employees by _____% and reduce yearly search fees from_____ to _____ in 20_____.
7) Reduce lawsuits and cut legal expenses from_____ to _____ in 20_____..

8) Increase wellness among employees and reduce medical expenses from_____ to _____ in 20_____..

9) Every employee will cut back on phone and e-mail time to family and friends each day by _____minutes in 20_____.

Goal Three- Meet the Expectations and Needs of Your Customers and Grow Your Customer Base

1) Retain existing customers and increase new customers by _____% in 20_____.

2) Identify three services or improvements in products that will retain our customers in 20_____.

3) Identify, develop, buy ____new products that will expand our customer base.

4) Design a customer satisfaction survey and assess customers twice per year making the appropriate changes to retain customers in 20_____.

5) Create five outrageous new services that will increase the customer base by _____% in 20_____.

6) Establish the Partnership Expectation PAC with customers inside and outside the company and honor each agreement in 20_____.

7) Send out a customer satisfaction survey three days after a service has been rendered and use the information to make the appropriate changes to retain customers in 20_____.

Goal Four -Recruit, Develop and Retain Employees Who Will Help You Be the Best in Your Industry

1) All employees must meet a minimum of 12 times a year with their team unit leader One-On-One to set and achieve the Best in Field objectives.

2) All employees must participate and attend 90% of the team unit meetings and achieve their Best in Field team unit objectives in 20_____..

3) All employees must develop a career path profile and resume so they can be placed in the right position in organization to complete tasks that help the unit meet its Best in Filed objectives in 20_____.

4) The One-On-One individual plan should include meeting the three most crucial needs of each employee in 20_____.

5) The One-On-One Best in Field objectives should address three areas where individuals are most dissatisfied and eliminate them in 20_____

6) The One-On-One meetings between team leader and team member will discuss the topics of change, stress and anxiety and how each individual can better manage these issues in 20_____.

7) Each employee must be an expert performer at:

  - Setting objectives and identifying the tasks needed to be complete to meet the objectives.
  - Technical knowledge and skills
  - Career planning, development and placement
  - Operating as a performance facilitator to others
  - Understanding group dynamics and how teams succeed and fail

8) Each employee will participate in the TASK Expert Process so they can become an expert performer at their position and move to another position if a colleague leaves the organization.

9) Each employee will be expected to participate in the Triangle Team Leadership Model and help fellow team members, the department, division and company achieve their Best in Field objectives.

Goal Five- *Build a Performance Facilitating Culture, One That Brings Out The Best In Others to Be Best in Our Field*

1) 100% of employees should review the company vision and mission statements, discuss them, and commit to them in 20_____.

2) At least 90% of the employees should approve the corporate growth goals and Best in Field objectives and commit to them in 20_____.

3) The Best in Our Filed objectives should be established and met by everyone on the team in 20_____.

4) All executives, managers and supervisors must learn the *Triangle Team Leadership Model* and how to be effective in the One-On-One and team unit meetings to transform reports into expert task performers.

5) Each team unit will adopt a number of guiding themes that will take the unit as far and high as they want to go.

6) The company will develop a number of performance facilitating behaviors and have each person on the team turn them in to every day habits. Each person will be evaluated on these behaviors in One-On-One meetings with their team unit leader twice a year and during their team unit meetings.

7) Performance facilitating work rules (bringing out the best in each other) should be written and carried out to facilitate performance, build a positive work environment and retain employees.

8) Everyone in the organization will be assessed as a skilled helper and performance facilitator and trained as one in the year 20_____.

Goal Six- Meet the Expectations of Your Shareholders

1) Increase dividends to stock holders from_____ to _____ in 20_____.
2) Meet the earnings projections, and develop a strategy to sell the stock analysts and public on buying company stock so it goes from _____ to _____ in 20_____.

Goal Seven- Meet the Expectations of Your Suppliers

1) Identify the three expectations of suppliers, develop a plan and meet them in 20_____.
2) Meet with your suppliers _____ times per year to establish rapport and give them an evaluation report on their products and services.
3) Pay your suppliers within _____days so they don't go out of business.

Goal Eight- Meet the Needs and Expectations of Family Members

1) Identify the two most crucial needs of family members, develop a plan and meet these needs in 20_____.
2) Identify what spouses, and children expect from those team members married and meet these expectations in 20_____.
3) Develop a "Mentoring Our Millennials Program" at work to help parents be more effective in helping their children succeed in school, life and work and be out the house by 30.

Goal Nine- Meet the Expectations and Needs of Retired Employees

1) Identify the two most crucial needs of retired employees, develop a plan and meet these needs in 20_____.
2) Identify where you need help in your company and hire _____ retired employees.
3) Identify what your retired employees expect from you and try to meet these expectations in 20_____.
4) If you establish a company mentoring program, hire _____ retirees to serve as mentors in 20_____.

Goal Ten- Help the Local Community in a Positive Way

1) Each employee will participate in one community project in 20_____.
2) Make a list of actions that your company could do to help your local community in 20_____ and select two that you would like to do.
3) Participate in ____school programs and help students understand your industry.

Goal Eleven- Identify the Strengths of Each Direct Report and Develop a Plan For Them to Use Their Strengths to Meet their Best in Our Field Objectives

1) Team members should participate in the Team Engagement Achievement Motivation (TEAM) Program and identify each person's strengths on the team based on their past successes.
2) Each team member should fill out _____ relevant assessment surveys so they and the team leader can chart their career journey.

Goal Twelve- Identify the Weaknesses of Each Direct Report and Create a Plan to Transform the Identified Weaknesses into Strengths.

1) The team members will go through the *Task Expert Process* and identify weaknesses that need to be improved..
2) The team members will take a number of relevant assessments and identify their weaknesses and develop a plan to turn the weaknesses into strengths.

Goal Thirteen--Meet Expectations of Work Colleagues and Fellow Department Heads

1) You will identify and meet with important work colleagues and with fellow department heads outside your department and draw up a *Partner Expectation Pac* with a list of what you can expect from each other .
2) You will meet quarterly with these important work colleagues and department heads and grade yourselves on how you are meeting each others expectations.

What other goals should your organization establish today? Write below.

<u>Notes</u>

Quote

"The defining characteristic of a true leader is that he or she never accepts the world as it is but instead always strives to make the world as it should be"

Condoleeza Rice

Section Two

The Team Leader Analysis & Improvement Program

Task One-

Defining Leadership and Management

According to research at the Human Resources Institute [ii] of Eckland College in St. Petersburg, Florida, the development of leaders has been a tremendous challenge for companies for the past ten years and will continue to be well into the 21st century. The Human Resources Institute conducted a worldwide study with 312 companies and the results are below.

The Important Issues Impacting People Management around the World in the Next 10 Years

Ranked by Overall Mean Response (n=312)
Key: 1=Extremely Important;   2=Somewhat Important;
       3=Important;   4=Not Important

	Overall		*U.S.*		*Europe*		*Asia*	
	Rank	Mean	Rank	Mean	Rank	Mean	Rank	Mean
Information technology	1	1.27	2	1.25	6	1.33	1	1.28
Leadership	2	1.28	1	1.25	9	1.42	5	1.36
Focus on the customer	3	1.29	3	1.28	4	1.27	6	1.36
Skill level of workforce	4	1.34	4	1.35	3	1.21	16	1.56
Managing change	5	1.38	5	1.39	1	2.21	8	1.42
Electronic transfer of info	6	1.43	6	1.46	2	1.21	7	1.38
The information superhighway	7	1.48	7	1.50	5	1.27	9	1.44
Innovation & creativity	8	1.51	8	1.53	10	1.42	12	1.48
Improving productivity	9	1.55	9	1.55	30	1.75	11	1.48
Quality of technical education	10	1.55	13	1.59	16	1.55	4	1.36
Employee communication	11	1.56	10	1.55	20	1.64	20	1.60
Intranet	12	1.59	16	1.61	12	1.46	21	1.60
Enhancing quality	13	1.60	12	1.58	25	1.67	23	2.68
Quality of primary education	14	1.60	11	1.56	28	1.73	32	1.79
Countries' global competitiveness	15	1.64	22	1.74	7	1.38	2	1.32
HR information systems	16	1.65	18	1.68	21	1.64	14	1.52
The learning organization	17	1.66	17	1.64	17	1.61	25	1.75
Quality of higher education	18	1.67	19	1.69	26	1.70	26	1.75
Healthcare costs	19	1.71	15	1.60	61	2.22	40	1.92
Ethics in business	20	1.71	20	1.72	31	1.76	27	1.76

Managing strategic alliances	21	1.75	27	1.81	13	1.50	19	1.60
Rate of economic growth	22	1.77	24	1.78	23	1.67	33	1.83
U.S. competition	23	1.78	14	1.60	38	1.97	75	2.57
Business information software	24	1.78	26	1.80	33	1.79	24	1.72
Quality of work life	25	1.79	28	1.82	24	1.67	29	1.76

The companies in the United States ranked <u>Leadership #1</u>, while European companies ranked <u>Managing Change as #1</u>. Asian companies ranked <u>Information Technology as #1</u>.

An article entitled "**The Leadership Industry**" [iii] (*Fortune* magazine, Feb. 21, 2009) stated that over 600 institutions offer some formal approach to leadership. In the article, Professor James O' Toole, head of a corporate leadership forum at the Aspen Institute, says, "people were having trouble selling their management ideas under their own labels, so they started calling it leadership." The article also says that Tom Peters, co-author of *In Search of Excellence* is paid $55,000 for speaking one to two hours, or $80,000 a day. A company's willingness to pay such fees illustrates the importance of leadership to today's organizations.

Asking employees what effective leaders do elicits a variety of answers such as:

- ➤ **Establish the vision or mission**
- ➤ **Motivate and inspire**
- ➤ **Set a strategy**
- ➤ **Responsible for results**

Still, the definition of effective leadership eludes many organizations. Warren G. Bennis, educator and author, defines leadership as "the capacity to translate vision into reality."[1] He states that the challenge of leadership is to create a social architecture where ideas, relationships and adventure can flourish. He adds that leaders know who they are; their strengths and weaknesses. They use their strengths and compensate for their weaknesses. They know what they want and why, and how to communicate that in order to gain cooperation and support. Finally, they know how to achieve their goal. Bennis suggests three basic reasons why leaders are important:

1) They are responsible for the effectiveness of the organization.
2) They serve as anchors in an organization thus providing stability.
3) They bring integrity to an organization allowing those doing business together to trust one another.

In his book, *The Leadership Factor,* [iv.] John Kotter contends that leadership is the same for a CEO as it is for a project leader ten layers lower in the company. He defines effective leadership as:

1) Setting a change agenda/vision of what can be; a vision which takes into account the legitimate interests of everyone involved.
2) A strategy for achieving the vision that takes into account all the organizational and environmental forces
3) Building a strong implementation network, an alliance or coalition powerful enough to implement the strategy.
4) Recruiting/selecting a highly motivated group of influential key people in the network who are committed to making the vision a realty.

Kotter further states "there is a growing need for leadership at all levels." Corporations worldwide are discovering that they need more people who can help them combat the economic warfare created by increased competition. Lower level managerial, professional and technical employees need to play a leadership role in their areas. No matter what the size of a company, it is essential that the CEO have everyone lead in different ways."

What to Look for in Leaders

John Kotter described the following as the requirements needed for providing effective leadership:

1) An inborn need to achieve is motivated by challenge and a strong drive to lead.
2) Strong personal values – a high degree of integrity and honesty.
3) Possessing the ability, keen mind and strong interpersonal skills.
4) An excellent reputation and track record in a broad set of activities.
5) A broad set of solid relationships in the firm and in the industry.
6) Broad knowledge of the industry and company.

Kotter described the attributes needed in lower & middle management leadership:

- Require an understanding of the position; a broader knowledge than just the technical requirements of the job
- The ability to develop a working relationship with others
- A track record and reputation of being credible
- A minimum set of intellectual and interpersonal skills
- Integrity and honesty
- Minimum energy level and a desire to lead

John Kotter outlined the differences between management and leadership in another book titled, *A Force for Change: How Leadership Differs from Management, 1999*. Kotter states that management and leadership are not mutually exclusive. A team leader needs to develop the appropriate background and skills to be effective in both areas. A combination of effective leadership and good management can provide structure and encourage innovation to bring out the best in everyone. The differences are outlined below.

	(Planning)	**(Vision)**
Creating An Agenda	Establishing detailed steps and timetables for achieving needed results and then developing a budget to make it happen.	Developing a vision of the future agenda and strategies for producing the changes needed to achieve that vision.
	(Organizing and Staffing)	**(Aligning People)**
Developing A Human Network For Achieving The Agenda	Establishing an organization structure for accomplishing results, selecting the right people, delegating authority for carrying out the plan, providing policies and procedures to guide people and creating systems to implement the plans	Communicating the direction by words and deeds to all those whose cooperation may be needed, influencing the creation of teams and coalitions that understand and believe in the vision and strategies and accept their validity
	(Controlling and Problem Solving)	**(Motivating and inspiring)**
Execution	Monitoring the step by step plan, making modifications in the plan, and solving problems	Energizing people to overcome obstacles (politics, negatives resource barriers) and meeting unfulfilled human needs
	(Obtaining Results)	**(Anticipating & Managing Change)**
Outcomes	Key to meeting the results that senior management and all the stakeholders want from the company	Learns what changes the company needs to make to be profitable (new products that customers want, new approaches to labor relations)

Dr. Mulligan places people into two leadership roles - **The Team Unit Leader** and **The Team Member Leader**.

The Team Unit Leader is classified as someone that leads, manages and mentors others. He/she must be able to establish predetermine objectives with direct reports and work with and through them to achieve the objectives within a given timeline. The team unit leader's challenge is to develop a common cause and objectives that will unite, motivate and reward everyone on the team. A common cause or an appropriate mission statement will pull everyone together to achieve the objectives. This person strives to be <u>an expert</u> in working with and through people implementing certain tasks to achieve specific objectives that will benefit all.

The Team Member Leader is responsible for managing only himself but still must be a team player. This person strives to be <u>an expert</u> in a functional area or at implementing specific tasks: engineer, programmer, accountant, sales person, researcher, underwriter, security person etc. They later are recognized in their organization as an expert leader in a special area performing certain tasks.

Some individuals like to manage a team of people or the entire organization and there are others who do not care to manage anyone but themselves. Many outstanding salespeople like to work on their own. Senior Executives want team unit leaders/ managers to work with and through their people to achieve the company objectives. Senior Executives strive to establish the vision, objectives and strategy while team unit leaders/managers are expected to execute the business plan so the company makes profit.

According to a study by Korn/Ferry,[vi] the leadership styles that made Senior Leaders the most successful were their social and participative leadership styles. While for team unit leaders/managers, it was their task-focus leadership styles. This reinforces the fact that Senior Executives expect team unit leaders (managers and supervisors) to drive the troops to achieve the business plan.

For people to be a expert team unit or team member leader, they must eventually be empowered or given **position power** (authority). One might be given a lot of responsibility, but without position power or authority, it is difficult to obtain the results doing it your way. The more authority you are given the more freedom you have to develop and implement your own plan and do it the way you think it should be done. It is difficult to be held accountable for completing a plan when you do not have the authority.

Team unit leaders should meet one on one with their direct reports and develop objectives, action plans and tasks that need to be completed. **Position power** can then be given to direct reports on tasks that they are able and willing to do. They then become expert leaders on certain tasks or areas in the organization. **Position power** is increased as one is recognized as an expert in a specific skill or task area. A team unit and team member leader should also learn how to develop their **personal power.** This is learning how to build rapport with others and operate as a helper/performance facilitator. Leaders need to work on their personal power first and then work with their boss to gain more position power. Leadership by example (positive behavior) build one's **personal and position power.**

Dr. Mulligan says team unit leaders also need <u>excellent management skills</u> in the areas of planning, organizing, directing, coordinating and controlling to be successful. Management is defined as setting pre-determined objectives with your direct reports and working with and through them to meet the objectives.

Functions of Management

Planning and Budgeting

What are we aiming for and how much will it cost us to accomplish it?

Organizing

Who is involved and how?

Directing

Who is doing what and when?

Coordinating

Who informs who and about what?

Controlling

Who judges the results and by what standards?

Copyright © 2018 Michael V. Mulligan

Korn/ Ferry International, a management placement firm, surveyed 1,500 senior leaders in 2006 to describe the key traits needed by CEOs to take them to the year 2010. The four top ingredients necessary for a leader, according to the survey, were:

- **Vision**
- **Strategic skills**
- **Able to move quickly**
- **Picking the right individuals to be on the team**

The June 21, 2009 Fortune magazine profiled a "Superior CEO" [vii] as possessing: ***Integrity, maturity and energy*-** The foundation on which everything is built.

- *Business acumen-* A deep understanding of the business and a strong profit orientation – an almost instinctive feel for how the company makes money.
- **People acumen-**Judging, leading teams, growing and coaching people; cutting losses where necessary.
- **Organization acumen-** Engendering trust, sharing information and listening expertly; diagnosing whether the organization is performing at full potential; delivering on commitments; changing, not just running, the business; being decisive and confident.
- **Curiosity, intellectual capacity and a global mindset-**Being externally oriented and hungry for knowledge of the world; adept at connecting developments and spotting patterns.
- **Superior judgment.**
- **An insatiable appetite for accomplishment and results.**
- **A powerful motivation to grow and convert learning into practice.**
- **Effective communication skills.**

Does Age Matter When You are a CEO?

There was a cover story in the August 13, 2008 edition of USA Todayasking the question "Does age matter when you are a CEO?" Spencer Stuart stated in the article that the median age for an S&P 500 CEO in 2007 was 55. Spencer Stuart went on to say that companies are gravitating toward the sweet-spot age of 55.Since the year 2000, the percentage of S&P 500 CEO's 50 to 59 has increased to %58 from %53. Spencer Stuart went on to report that among today's S&P 500 CEO's, 27 (5.4%) are 47 and younger and six (1.2%) are 72 and older. The question in hiring a CEO is energy vs. wisdom. The article went on to say that the youngest CEOs had better performance than older CEOs but not significantly.

What Derails Leaders in their Company- Fatal Flaws[viii]

M. W. McCall, Jr., and M. M. Lombardo wrote a technical report in June 2008 entitled, "Off the Track: Why and How Successful Executives Get Derailed."

1) Specific performance problems with the business – this person can't handle certain parts of the business and fails to admit the problem. He or she covers it up, blames others and shows that they can't change.
2) Insensitivity to others – an abrasive, intimidating, bully-style of behavior.
3) Cold, aloof and arrogant – some managers are so brilliant that they become arrogant and intimidate others with their knowledge. This person makes others feel stupid, doesn't listen, and has all the answers.
4) Betrayal of trust – this is where a manager commits what is perhaps a manager's only forgivable sin. They betray a trust. Some people use information about others as power and use it for their own good. The failure to follow through on promises also creates havoc.
5) Over managing – failing to delegate, empower or build a team that can handle operational activities. At the executive level, it's fatal because you have a staff of self-managers who want to be in charge and do it their way.
6) Overly ambitious – thinking of the next job, playing politics. People bruise others and spend too much time pleasing upper management.
7) Failing to staff effectively – some managers get along with their staff but have the wrong people in the job. They staff in their own image and don't release people quickly enough when they perform poorly.
8) Inability to think strategically – preoccupied with detail – can't hit the numbers which is the number one reason for failure. They can't go from being doers to being planners.
9) Unable to adapt to a boss with a different style. This situation can cause a person to get into wars over different opinions and be unhappy at work.
10) Over-dependence on a mentor or advocate. Sometimes managers stay with a single advocate or mentor too long.

Strategic Leadership

John C. Maxwell wrote *Developing the Leaders Around You.*[ix] He makes a number of suggestions on how leaders can help others reach their full potential.

- Study the art of directing people: know how to lead, direct, manage.
- Study ahead of your people: leadership is drive. Lead by pace setting. Work harder and smarter than your staff. See the problems first and think ahead to solutions.
- Study the art of persuasion: learn how to bring people to your way of thinking. Apply sales psychology in leadership the same as you do in selling.
- Seek your direct reports advice: ask for their opinions. Encourage them to express themselves. Consult with them and accept their ideas. Don't think you know all the angles.
- See their viewpoints: learn to listen to their problems. Hear them out, even when you don't agree. Try to walk in their shoes.
- Help them to see your viewpoint: explain your point of view better, don't just state it. Justify and support it. Give your reasons. The will help you and cooperate more readily if they know the background and reasons for your decision.
- Make sure your direct reports follow through on plans and do the best they can.
- Face unpleasantness frankly: air troubles. Have bull sessions when necessary. Permit and encourage suggestions when things aren't going smoothly.
- Hold meetings often and regularly.
- Build the concept if the team succeeds, we all succeed.
- Let each person know what to expect and where they stand; do not fail to discuss his/her performance with him/her periodically.
- Keep your antennae up always trying to detect changes in the market place and make plans accordingly.

Task Two

Establish Leadership Behaviors for Team Members and Conduct 360 Degree Leadership Surveys to Measure and Change Behaviors

As you start your new position and have a business plan in place, it is important for you to let your direct reports know how important it is for everyone to step up as a leader. However, you want everyone to have a buy in to what leadership behaviors you should implement the most to achieve the business plan. Therefore, you should ask your direct reports to work with you to identify the seven or eight behaviors that are crucial in helping the organization be successful.

Management Research Group created the 360 degree *Strategic Leadership Program* [x] that can be used to help the team identify the top eight to 10 leadership behaviors most crucial to helping the company be successful. The program has three stages. In **stage one,** each direct report will fill out a leadership questionnaire reviewing 22 leadership behaviors (see next page). A report will comeback showing how each person rated the leadership behaviors.

In **stage two,** each team member will review their report showing how he/she rated the 22 leadership behaviors and how the team as a whole rated the 22 leadership behaviors. You as the team unit leader can then sit down with all your direct reports and try to reach consensus on what leadership behaviors should be emphasized more than others even though they all are important. This will give you a chance to learn how each direct report values certain leadership behaviors.

In **stage three**, all team leaders will have others fill out a *360 Leadership Analysis Survey* on them to learn how they are viewed in implementing the 22 leadership behaviors, especially the eight to 10 most important behaviors selected by the group. If a team unit leader or team member leader receives low scores on certain leadership behaviors, he/she should develop a plan to improve themselves in this area. *A 360 Leadership Analysis Survey* will be completed every four months to make sure everyone is doing well in implementing the behaviors.

Leadership Development Program

The *Management Research Group* in Portland Maine[2] has developed a *360 degree leadership evaluation program* to help organizations develop the strategic leadership practices that will help them be competitive and successful. The program asks the organization leaders to identify the eight to 10 leadership behaviors, if emulated, would take the organization forward. Then a 360 degree survey is passed out to those who work with each team unit leader. The results are tallied and interpreted to each leader. Each team unit leader is asked to develop a development plan to improve his/her leadership practices. The program helps the leaders practice those leadership behaviors that will make them and the company be successful. The 22 Leadership Behaviors that are measured in the 360 degree survey are listed and described below. Please rate yourself on the 22 behaviors using the following 5.0 evaluation scale.

5-Definitely like me   **4- Usually like me**   **3- Somewhat like me**
2- A little like me   **1- Not like me**

Write in the number by the leadership practice that best fits your behavior at this time. The 22 leadership practices are divided into six areas.

1) **Creating a Vision**
   _____**Conservative**- You study problems in light of past practices to ensure predictability, reinforce the status quo and minimize risk.
   _____**Innovative**- You feel comfortable in fast-changing environments, being willing to take risks and to consider new and untested approaches.
   _____**Technical**- You acquire and maintain in-depth knowledge in your field or areas of focus; using your expertise and special knowledge to study issues in depth and draw conclusions.
   _____**Self**- You emphasize the importance of making decisions independently; looking to yourself as the prime vehicle for decision-making.
   _____**Strategic**- You take a long range, broad approach to problem solving and decision making through objective analysis, thinking ahead and planning.

2) **Developing Fellowship**
   _____**Persuasive**- You build commitment by convincing others and winning them over to your point of view.
   _____**Outgoing**- You act in an extroverted, friendly and informal manner; showing a capacity to quickly establish free and easy interpersonal relationships.
   _____**Excitement**-You operate with a good deal of energy, intensity and emotional expression; having a capacity for keeping others enthusiastic and involved.
   _____**Restraint**- You maintain a low-key, understated and quite interpersonal demeanor by working to control your emotional expressions.

3) **Implementing The Vision**

_____**Structuring-** You adopt a systematic and organized approach; preferring to work in a precise, methodical manner; developing and using guidelines and procedures.

_____**Tactical-** You emphasize the production of immediate results by focusing on short-range, hands-on, practical strategies.

_____**Communication-** You state clearly what you want and expect from others; clearly expressing your thoughts and ideas; maintaining a precise and constant flow of information.

_____**Delegation-** You enlist the talents of others to help meet objectives by giving them important activities and sufficient autonomy to exercise their own judgment.

4) **Following Through**

_____**Control-** You adopt an approach in which you take nothing for granted. You set deadlines for certain actions and are persistent in monitoring the progress of activities to insure that they are completed on schedule.

_____**Feedback-** You let others know in a straightforward manner on how well they have performed and if they have met your needs and expectations.

5) **Achieving Results**

_____**Management Focus-** You seek to exert influence by being in positions of authority, taking charge and leading and directing the efforts of others.

_____**Dominant-** You push vigorously to achieve results through an approach which is forceful, assertive and competitive.

_____**Productive-** You adopt a strong orientation toward achievement; holding high expectations for yourself and others and pushing a high standard.

6) **Team Playing**

_____**Cooperative-** You accommodate the needs and interests of others by helping them achieve their objectives.

_____**Consensual-** You value the ideas and opinions of others and collect their input as part of your decision-making process.

_____**Authority Oriented-** You show loyalty to the organization by respecting the ideas and opinions of people in authority and using them as resources for information, direction and decisions.

_____**Empathy-** You demonstrate an active concerned for people and their needs by forming close supportive relationships with others.

Reviewing Your Perceived Leadership Strengths and Weaknesses

(Strengths)

List the <u>Topics</u> You Answered 5

List the <u>Topics</u> You Answered 4

(Need Improvement0

List the <u>Topics</u> You Answered 3

(Really Need Improvement)

List the <u>Topics</u> You Answered 2

List the <u>Topics</u> You Answered 1

Contact Management Research Group or Mulligan & Associates if you want to do a 360 degree *Strategic Leadership Program* in your organization.

Task Three

The Mulligan Leadership Personality Profile

Read each phrase below and evaluate the degree to which the phrase <u>describes you</u>.
Please answer all 80 items using the following rating system.

Rating Scale

6. Statement is <u>definitely</u> like me   5. Statement is <u>very much</u> like me

4. Statement is <u>somewhat</u> like me   3. Statement is <u>partially</u> like me

2. Statement is <u>rarely</u> like me   1. Statement is <u>definitely not</u> like me

1) I have a high want to achieve and be successful.	6	5	4	3	2	1
2) I don't accept rejection easily.	6	5	4	3	2	1
3) I can work alone and account for my actions.	6	5	4	3	2	1
4) I weigh all the options carefully before making decisions.	6	5	4	3	2	1
5) I take things as they come and don't panic.	6	5	4	3	2	1
6) I am an approachable person.	6	5	4	3	2	1
7) I am a strategic thinker-future oriented and look at big picture.	6	5	4	3	2	1
8) I promote team cohesiveness.	6	5	4	3	2	1
9) I am a competitive person.	6	5	4	3	2	1
10) I have a high will to achieve and be successful.	6	5	4	3	2	1
11) I march to my own drum beat.	6	5	4	3	2	1
12) I work hard to avoid making mistakes.	6	5	4	3	2	1
13) I am cool under fire and keep my composure.	6	5	4	3	2	1
14) I am a good sounding board for others.	6	5	4	3	2	1
15) I like to brainstorm and improve the way of doing things.	6	5	4	3	2	1
16) I am a person who genuinely cares about others.	6	5	4	3	2	1
17) I am an aggressive person.	6	5	4	3	2	1
18) I am determined to achieve the objectives I set for myself.	6	5	4	3	2	1
19) I am my own person.	6	5	4	3	2	1
20) I am organized.	6	5	4	3	2	1
21) I can control my emotions when under pressure.	6	5	4	3	2	1
22) I am a good listener always focusing on what is being said.	6	5	4	3	2	1
23) I am process improvement oriented, making things better.	6	5	4	3	2	1

24) I encourage the acceptance of individual differences   6   5   4   3   2   1

25) I have a sense of urgency in getting things done.   6   5   4   3   2   1

26) I apply myself to the fullest to complete a task.   6   5   4   3   2   1

27) I stand my ground when I think I am right.   6   5   4   3   2   1

28) I am very thorough when working on tasks and projects.   6   5   4   3   2   1

29) I can control my temper.   6   5   4   3   2   1

30) I help people improve themselves at what they do.   6   5   4   3   2   1

31) I am recognized as someone who has good ideas.   6   5   4   3   2   1

32) I promote coordination of effort between people.   6   5   4   3   2   1

33) I don't like to lose when I am in a competitive situation.   6   5   4   3   2   1

34) I move fast to take advantage of new opportunities.   6   5   4   3   2   1

35) I have a mind of my own.   6   5   4   3   2   1

36) I am detail oriented.   6   5   4   3   2   1

37) I stay objective when being attacked by others   6   5   4   3   2   1

38) I am effective at helping and coaching others.   6   5   4   3   2   1

39) I am creative.   6   5   4   3   2   1

40) I promote setting boundaries between people.   6   5   4   3   2   1

41) I make things happen.   6   5   4   3   2   1

42) I strive to be the best at what I do.   6   5   4   3   2   1

43) I can fend for myself.   6   5   4   3   2   1

44) I am sharp as a tack as nothing gets past me.   6   5   4   3   2   1

45) I am even temperament and steady as a rock.   6   5   4   3   2   1

46) I call pe.ople by their name & acknowledge their presence.   6   5   4   3   2   1

47) I like to think situations out before taking action   6   5   4   3   2   1

48) I promote team play.   6   5   4   3   2   1

49) I set high standards for myself and others.   6   5   4   3   2   1

50) I am driven.   6   5   4   3   2   1

51) I prefer to do things my way.   6   5   4   3   2   1

52) I leave no stone unturned   6   5   4   3   2   1

53) I am patient and self disciplined.   6   5   4   3   2   1

54) I reward people for doing what they say they will do   6   5   4   3   2   1

55) I am a curious about how things work and operate.   6   5   4   3   2   1

56) I like to work in a collaborative work environment.   6   5   4   3   2   1

57) I like to be in control and charge of a situation.   6   5   4   3   2   1

58) I move quickly to get things done.   6   5   4   3   2   1

59) I am strong minded.   6   5   4   3   2   1

60) I am technically oriented   6   5   4   3   2   1

61) I believe haste can make waste.   6   5   4   3   2   1

62) I confront those who don't walk their talk.   6   5   4   3   2   1

63) I am a critical thinker.	6	5	4	3	2	1
64) I use positive reinforcement to motivate team mates.	6	5	4	3	2	1
65) I possess an entrepreneurial spirit.	6	5	4	3	2	1
66) I am persistent and see things through to the end.	6	5	4	3	2	1
67) I am a self starter.	6	5	4	3	2	1
68) I am good at gathering facts and investigating situations.	6	5	4	3	2	1
69) I am calm and steady when placed in a negotiating situation.	6	5	4	3	2	1
70) I am effective at bringing out the best in people.	6	5	4	3	2	1
71) I am good at solving problems.	6	5	4	3	2	1
72) I promote team play.	6	5	4	3	2	1
73) I push myself and others to the limit.	6	5	4	3	2	1
74) I am an intense person who likes to be the best	6	5	4	3	2	1
75) I am independent.	6	5	4	3	2	1
76) I am a good researcher and investigator.	6	5	4	3	2	1
77) I am exceptionally poised during heated discussions.	6	5	4	3	2	1
78) I am empathic and respectful toward others	6	5	4	3	2	1
79) I anticipate changes and prepare myself to manage them	6	5	4	3	2	1
80) I believe that you win when you work together as a team.	6	5	4	3	2	1

Calculate Your Scores for Each of the Eight Personality Traits

Listed below are eight personality traits. There are 10 phrases on the survey for each trait. Please go back to the survey and review your answer on each statement. If you scored a 6, place 15 points by the statement number below; if your scored a 5, place 12 points by the statement number below; if you scored a 4, place 9 points on the statement number below; if you scored a 3, place 6 points on the statement number below; if you scored a 2, place 3 points on the statement number below and if you scored a 1, place 0 points by the statement number below. Then add up all the points to learn your total score for that particular personality trait. Write your total score 0 to 150 for each trait on the following page and identify the level 1 to 5 where you perceive yourself functioning at this time.

Competitiveness/Aggressiveness (High Want to Achieve)

1____ 9____ 17____ 25____ 33____ 41____ 49____ 57____ 65____ 73____
Total Points _____

Determined/Persistent (High Will to Achieve)

2____ 10____ 18____ 26____ 34____ 42____ 50____ 58____ 66____ 74____
Total Points _____

Self Directed/Independent (Can Do It Alone)

3____ 11____ 19____ 27____ 35____ 43____ 51____ 59____ 67____ 75____
Total Points _____

Thorough//Detailed/ Investigative(On Top of Things – Hands-On Practical Thinker)

4____ 12____ 20____ 28____ 36____ 44____ 52____ 60____ 68____ 76____
Total Points _____

Patient/Self Control (Stay Cool Under Fire)

5____ 13____ 21____ 29____ 37____ 45____ 53____ 61____ 69____ 77____
Total Points _____

Helper/Performance Facilitator (Help Others Solve Their Own Problem and Grow)

6____ 14____ 22____ 30____ 38____ 46____ 54____ 62____ 70____ 78____
Total Points _____

Innovative/Creative/Strategic (Always Trying to Improve Your Situation &Organization)

7____   15____   23____   31____   39____   47____   55____   63____   71____   79____
Total Points _____

Team Builder and Player (Always Pulling the Team Together)

8____   16____   24____   32____   40____   48____   56____   64____   72____   80____
Total Points _____

Copyright © 2018 Michael V. Mulligan

Review Your Scores and Functioning Level on Eight Personality Traits

We have combined your eighty answers into eight personality traits. Your total points should be placed in the right column below. Based on your total score, you will fall into one of five levels. The higher your total points and level, the more you are like the trait. The lower your total points and level, the less likely you resemble the trait. The score range is 0 to 150. Keep in mind that this profile represents the perceptions you have of yourself and is not a test of right and wrong answers.

(Review on the following pages how you would probably behave based on your personality trait scores)

	150	120	90	60	30	0	
Eight Personality Measures	Definitely Like You	Usually Like You	Somewhat Like You	A Little Like You	Not Like You	Scores
Competitive- A High Want to Achieve and be # 1	Level 5	Level 4	Level 3	Level 2	Level 1	
Determined- A High Will to Achieve and be # 1	Level 5	Level 4	Level 3	Level 2	Level 1	
Self-Directed/ Independent	Level 5	Level 4	Level 3	Level 2	Level 1	
Thorough/ Detailed Technical	Level 5	Level 4	Level 3	Level 2	Level 1	
Patient/Self Control	Level 5	Level 4	Level 3	Level 2	Level 1	
Helpful/ Performance Facilitator	Level 5	Level 4	Level 3	Level 2	Level 1	
Innovative Creative Strategic (See Big Picture)	Level 5	Level 4	Level 3	Level 2	Level 1	
Team Builder/ TeamPlayer	Level 5	Level 4	Level 3	Level 2	Level 1	
	150	120	90	60	30	0	

(Left vertical label: "TRAITS")

If you fall at level 5 or at Level 4 with a score of 90 and above, your behavior is more like the trait being described. A Level 3 places you in the average range of likeness. If you fall at Level 1 or 2 with a score of 60 or less, you view yourself somewhat opposite of the trait being described. This information can help you see where you need to step up your behavior when operating in a team unit leader and team member leader role.

Competitive /Aggressive Trait©

Competitive/ Aggressive-A high want to be number one

Personality Measure	Definitely Like You	Usually Like You	Somewhat Like You	A Little Like You	Not Like You	Score
Competitive- A high want to succeed.	Level 5	Level 4	Level 3	Level 2	Level 1	

	←	←	←	←	←	←
Range	150	120	90	60	30	0

The higher your score and level, the more:

- You have a <u>high want to succeed</u> and be # one.
- You want to determine the vision, the strategies and the growth objectives of the unit/organization.
- You want to align the organization and select the people who will execute the growth plan.
- You are driven, competitive, aggressive and entrepreneurial.
- You would like to determine the services and products to sell and the customer base.
- You would establish a high standard for yourself and those who report to you and expect everyone to meet the standards that are in place.
- You are motivated by challenge.
- You like to be in control.
- You would like to help establish policies, procedures, structure for everyone to follow.
- You are likely to withstand higher levels of self-imposed pressure and longer duration of stress.
- You would criticize yourself and others when the performance is not at the level you want it to be.
- You might be argumentative, irritable and abrasive with others when things aren't going right.
- You would drive the team forward and meet the organization's vision and objectives.
- Your competitive spirit will generate energy in others.
- You would work hard to convince others to buy your product/service or ideas.
- You would prospect to find customers and money to support the unit/organization.

The Unit Leader/Manager-The competitive/aggressive trait is extremely important in being a unit leader and manager. You have to set performance objectives, that if met, will help your organization grow, be competitive and profitable and your unit be the best in it's functional area. You must ask team members to set and meet individual objectives that will help the team unit/organization meet it's objectives. A unit leader and manager has to be a self manager and being competitive is an important trait to possess.

Team members are asked to fill a leadership role that requires them to master and execute specific tasks. In essence, team members are asked to step us as expert leaders in a special work area that will help the unit/organization be successful. They have to be competitive and set their own performance objectives.

Sales Person-The salesperson is a team member who operates as a leader in his/ her assigned territory. Each team member (sales person) must meet his/her sales objective if the total organization is to be successful.

At what level are you functioning on the competitive scale above? At what level do you need to be functioning to be more effective in your present leadership role?

40

DETERMINED/PERSISTENT TRAIT©

Determined/ Persistent – a high will to be number one

Personality Measure	Definitely Like You	Usually Like You	Somewhat Like You	A Little Like You	Not Like You	Score
Determined- A high will to succeed.	Level 5	Level 4	Level 3	Level 2	Level 1	

Range	150	120	90	60	30	0

The higher your score and level, the more:

- You have a <u>high will to succeed</u> and be # one.
- You are persistent.
- You are determined and hard driving.
- You have a sense of urgency to achieve a task.
- You are eager and active in pursuing the completion of your task.
- You are focused.
- You would raise the energy and the intensity level of those around you.
- You would continuously pursue meeting an objective.
- You want to take the organization and people to greater heights.
- You would be an excellent closer when trying to sell something to a customer or an idea to a fellow employee during a meeting.
- Your boss and team mates/colleagues can depend on you to help them reach the objectives.

The *determined/persistent trait* is important in both leadership roles. If you are working in the unit leadership/ manager role, you have to start out setting achievable and believable objectives with team members. People must believe the objectives can be met and then they will work harder to achieve them. The unit leader/ manager should know each team member's determination and persistence level so the objectives they set are realistic to them. The unit leader and manager needs to develop an environment that motivates all team members to give it their all. If the team unit leader and manager is laid back and does not provide the intensity and energy to raise team members to greater performance heights, the team members need to step up to push their fellow employees.

A team member can raise the intensity level and performance of the team. Michael Jordan of the Chicago Bulls would not allow his team to quit when they got behind in a game. He talked to them, asked them to step it up another notch and willed the team to victory. Each team member must look at how determined, persistent and focused they are on achieving their own objectives as well as the team unit's objectives and then step it up a notch or two. The determination to win or be the best in one's field will help team unit's overcome a lack of talent and rise higher than one could ever expect.

At what level are you on the determined/ persistence scale above? At what level do you need to operate at to be successful in your present situation? At what level do you need to operate at to move to your next targeted position?

INDEPENDENT / SELF DIRECTED TRAIT©

Independent/Self Directed-prefer to manage oneself without supervision

Personality Measure	Definitely Like You	Usually Like You	Somewhat Like You	A Little Like You	Not Like You	Score
Independent/ Self-Directed	Level 5	Level 4	Level 3	Level 2	Level 1	

Range	150	120	90	60	30	0

The higher your score and level, the more:

- You like to work alone without supervision.
- You want authority and a wide range of freedom to develop and achieve your plan
- You would want the freedom to run your own show.
- You would like to be in charge of your own destiny.
- You are strong minded and firm in the way you do things.
- You are independent and self directed and would like working in an isolated team member role.
- You would have problems with an autocratic leader/domineering boss.
- You want to develop your own procedures and methods of doing business.
- You like planning, organizing and establishing your own day to day structure.
- You would be difficult to manage.
- You might have difficulty operating as a team player.
- You would have difficulty in following and being controlled by your boss.
- You would want to know the expectations of your boss.
- You would view yourself as a self- starter and self manager.
- You would want to manage self managers.
- You could operate on your own to sell products and services or work on a special project somewhere.

The *self directed/independent trait* is important in both leadership roles.. If you are working in the unit leadership/manager role, you want each team member to become a self manager and expert leader in his particular field so you can turn them loose without constantly supervising them. You can then spend more time monitoring the progress of the unit and communicating with others in the company and customers.

The team member leader needs to work on mastering his/her assigned tasks and meeting the objectives he/she and the boss set when the year first started. The team member needs to work on becoming a self manager so the boss empowers and provides complete authority to the person. One on One meetings between the unit leader/manager and team member can help the team member move to an expert leadership status and be empowered to operate on his/her own.

At what level are you on the self directed/independent scale above? At what level should you be to operate effectively in your present situation? What is your next targeted position and at what level do you need to be operating on the self directed scale to be successful in your next position?

DETAILED/THOROUGH/TECHNICAL TRAIT©

Detailed/Thorough/Technical-Nothing Gets Past Me/Very Practical

Personality Measure	Definitely Like You	Usually Like You	Somewhat Like You	A Little Like You	Not Like You	Score
Detailed/ Through/ Technical	Level 5	Level 4	Level 3	Level 2	Level 1	

	←	←	←	←	←	←
Range	150	120	90	60	30	0

The higher your score and level, the more:

- Your orientation would be toward detail, technical, factual, analytical and investigative work.
- You would enjoy solving intellectual challenges by investigating the facts and concepts associated with a problem or situation.
- You would take a cautious position toward making decisions. This behavior can help creative colleagues examine their ideas more thoroughly before make decisions that could be a costly.
- You might behave as an intellectual warrior and debate fellow employees so hard and long in a meeting that they might not want to meet with you again.
- You should use your technical orientation to good use.
- You would set up policies and procedures so people know how to operate in the organization.
- You would enjoy doing research and gathering facts to help the organization make wise decisions.
- You would make sure the organization was compliant with government and banking regulations and other pertinent rules set by the organization.
- You would work hard to keep the unit/organization under budget and profitable.
- Your boss would have confidence in assigning you tasks and listening to what you have to say.
- You would operate as a tactical strategist which requires day to day plans to get immediate results.

The *detailed/thorough/technical trait* is important in both leadership roles. If you are working in the unit leadership/manager role, you want to make sure you have done your homework when you hire people, set objectives and strategies and move forward to execute your plan. Unit/manager leaders need to understand new technology and be more into detail knowing the processes, procedures and policies set by the organization. This includes knowing the process and procedure to follow when recruiting, developing, promoting or

45

releasing someone. Organizations can spend more money than they need to spend each year on both search and litigation because unit leaders don't follow the rules set by their organization.

Senior leaders need to be more thorough when they purchase another company to expand market share. Many organizations have been hurt financially or gone out of business because they paid too much money on an acquisition. Unit leaders also need to be effective as a time manager today.

Team members need to be detailed and thorough in mastering their assigned tasks so the organization can be successful. Organizations depend on team member leaders to handle much of the detail and investigative work so the team unit leaders can develop realistic plans and long term and short term strategies. At what level did you place yourself on the detailed scale above? At what level should you operate to be effective in your present situation? What is your next position and at what level do you need to operate on the detailed scale to be effective?

PATIENT/SELF CONTROL ©

PATIENT/SELF CONTROL-NEVER LOSE MY COOL

Personality Measure	Definitely Like You	Usually Like You	Somewhat Like You	A Little Like You	Not Like You	Score
Patient/Self Control	Level 5	Level 4	Level 3	Level 2	Level 1	

| Range | 150 | 120 | 90 | 60 | 30 | 0 |

The higher score and level, the more:

- You would reflect a calm, steady, unhurried, relaxed, stable and patient manner.
- You can tolerate tasks that require longer periods of time to complete.
- You would take the time to learn about a person and thus be an effective helper or manager.
- You would spend the time transforming a direct report or colleague into a champion performer.
- You would listen to people for longer periods of time helping them explore and understand their situation before developing appropriate action steps.
- You would be viewed as approachable when one needs to talk about a problem.
- You would enjoy coaching employees taking them from the incompetent to the competent stage,
- You would keep your composure during intense discussions and not make hasty decisions.
- You would take things slowly and would not push the panic button.
- You would be mentally disciplined.
- You would be patient with customers and fellow workers.
- You would have to know when to push yourself and others into action when the need arises.

The ***Patient/Self Control trait*** is important in both leadership roles. If you are working in the unit leadership/ manager's role, you want to make sure you are patient and in self control at all times. When executives become angry and frustrated, they can make decisions that can come back to haunt them and the unit/organization. There have been stories about CEOs throwing pencils and swearing at their senior management staff as well as firing them on the spot because the sales numbers were not good. Unit leaders/managers need to work on their One on One Management skills and take the time to help direct reports / team members become expert leaders in their field. This takes patience and being in self control. As you rise in the management ranks, you don't expect to do as much coaching or be coached because you should already be an expert leader in your field and a self manager. However, you do need to be in control of your emotions. How many good decisions have you made when you were mad or angry?

Team member leaders need to be patient and in self control when their bosses and colleagues do and say stupid things. A study by Career Builder recently reported 30 % of the workers said they work for a bully. In an article in USA Today, 80 % of the workers said they participate in an uncivil like work environment. Team members need to be patient and in self control when working directly with obnoxious customers and each other. Employees helpful, patient and in self control with customers and fellow employees are a real asset to an organization. At what level of patience and self control did you place yourself on the above scale? At what level do you think you should be operating at today to be effective in your present situation? At what level do your need to operate on the self control scale to be effective in your next targeted position?

HELPER/PERFORMANCE FACILITATOR TRAIT©

Helper/Performance Facilitator-Bringing Out the Best in Those Around You

Personality Measure	Definitely Like You	Usually Like You	Somewhat Like You	A Little Like You	Not Like You	Score
Performance Facilitator and Helper	Level 5	Level 4	Level 3	Level 2	Level 1	

Range	150	120	90	60	30	0

The higher your score and level, the more:

- You would be someone a person would seek out to discuss and solve a problem or an issue.
- You would be perceived as a person who is caring and a good sounding board.
- You would help someone explore, understand and solve their situation without giving premature advice that could be harmful.
- You would have the capability to respond with empathy to a person who is in an unpleasant emotional state and move them to a logical state so they can think clearly and go back to work.
- You would help people establish, execute and meet growth objectives.
- You would be described as supportive and accepting of others.
- You would enjoy being in a position to take care of the behind the scenes work and keep the team on course to meet the objectives.
- You would enjoy managing and coaching people so they become a champion/expert leader in their field.
- You would like servicing customers and helping fellow colleagues in the organization.
- You would want to build a helping and performance facilitating work environment.
- You would spot talent in people and help them develop it.
- You would help people move toward their ultimate career position.
- You would build systems to identify talented people and grow them so the organization stays competitive and successful in the years ahead.
- You would confront someone if they are not walking their talk.
- You would challenge individuals to become the best they can be.
- You would set up and execute a leadership and performance management system in your unit/organization to help team members become champion/expert performers and the unit a championship organization.

The ***Helper/Performance Facilitator trait*** is important in both leadership roles. Everyone in an organization should go through a helping and performance facilitation training program. It is important for employees to learn how to build working relationships with each other, be able to focus listen and target respond when colleagues are talking in a One on One session or team meeting so in-depth understanding occurs and wise plans can be developed. If there are good working relationships built and employees help each other execute a well conceived plan, the team unit/organization will have a better chance of being successful. At what level did you place yourself on the helper/performance facilitator scale above? At what level do you need to operate effectively in your present and future position?

INNOVATIVE/CREATIVE/STRATEGIC TRAIT©

Innovative/Creative- An idea person who improves processes, products and service.

Personality Measure	Definitely Like You	Usually Like You	Somewhat Like You	A Little Like You	Not Like You	Score
Innovative/ Creative/ Strategic	Level 5	Level 4	Level 3	Level 2	Level 1	

Range	150	120	90	60	30	0

The higher your score and level, the more:

- You would operate as a visionary and strategic thinker, one who is always studying the landscape, sees the big picture and helps the organization become what it should become and be.
- You would like to brainstorm and come up with ideas that can help the unit/ organization.
- You would be looking to improve processes in the organization
- You would be a critical thinker, one who can digest, analyze and synthesize information and use the findings to make future plans..
- You would help people and your organization improve the way things are done.
- You would push people to think out of the box and be more innovative.
- You would like have the opportunity to be creative and work with ideas in your daily work.
- You would think things out before taking action.
- You would be curious about how things work.
- You would keep your antenna up to anticipate and make changes that are necessary.
- You would set up a system to keep up with the latest in your field so you can make improvements in your unit/organization.

The **Innovative/Creative/Strategic trait** is important in both leadership roles. If you are working in the unit leadership/manager's role, you want to make sure you work with others to create a vision of what the unit/organization should be like in the future and develop a plan to get there. The competition will continue to think of ways to be the best in the industry so your organization needs to tap it's brain power as well. Unit leadership needs to find the best minds and bring out the thinking of the present employees. Unit leaders also need to continue to think of how each department and the total organization can get better and stay ahead of the competition. Employees hear about continuous improvement but it needs to be practiced. Many employees have great ideas but no one solicits them.

When team unit leaders sit down to manage their direct reports One on One, this is the time to ask each person how they can improve what they are doing and how the unit and organization can be improved. Psychologists say people use about 15% of their potential. This is because many unit leaders look at their employees as grinders rather than asking them how they and the unit/organization can do things faster and better. There is an old saying "there is no one as smart as all of us". Unit leaders need to meet with direct reports and conduct "think tanks" to pull new and creative ideas out of them. Many team members need to also become tactical strategists creating practical step by step plans to help the organization reach it's destiny. At what level did you place yourself on the innovative/creative scale? At what level do you need to operate to be effective in your present situation or your next position?

TEAM BUILDER/ PLAYER©

TEAM BUILDER AND TEAM PLAYER- THERE IS NO ONE SMARTER THAN ALL OF US

Personality Measure	Definitely Like You	Usually Like You	Somewhat Like You	A Little Like You	Not Like You	Score
Team Builder/ Player	Level 5	Level 4	Level 3	Level 2	Level 1	

	←	←	←	←	←	←
Range	**150**	**120**	**90**	**60**	**30**	**0**

The higher your score, and level, the more:

- You would promote the sharing of ideas.
- You would concentrate on building team cohesiveness.
- You would reinforce continuous team play.
- You would create a collaborative and democratic work environment.
- You would want everyone on the planning team and being accountable for the results.
- You would encourage acceptance of differences of opinion and divergent thinking.
- You would promote acceptance of cultural and individual differences.
- You would increase emotional involvement in team objective achievement.
- You would put the spot light on the team and would wave the team flag.
- You would enjoy a close working relationship with your boss and team mates.
- You would want to review your job tasks with your boss and be sure of what he/she expects.
- You would want to execute the Triangle Team Leadership Model which will build team cohesiveness and transform the unit into a first class organization and members into leaders.

The *Team Builder/Player trait* is important in both leadership roles. If you are working in the unit leadership/manager's role, you want to make sure you communicate to your direct reports that it is people who play on championship teams that normally get ahead in the world. You can discuss the 1985 Chicago Bears team who won a super bowl. They not only won rings but obtained great jobs after their football days were over and still have good jobs today. You can also discuss the Miami Heat who presently have three super stars but don't know how to play as a team to win a world basketball championship.

People on team units need to know that if they play together, they and their unit/ organization can become the best at what they do. If this happens, their company will want to keep them and other companies will want to recruit them. Senior management likes to keep people who are talented and best in their field.

Another important point is that if you can build a strong working relationship with all the people that work in your unit and help each other and the unit be successful, there will be one person in the group whose career will take off. As that person moves up the management ladder, they will mostly likely take you with them. Your career can rise on the shirt tail of a fellow worker.

The Triangle Team Leadership Model: Becoming the Best in Our Field is a leadership and performance management system that can transform team members into expert leaders in their fields and the unit into a championship team. At what level did you place yourself on the team builder/player scale? At what level do you need to operate to be successful in your present or a future situation?

"Before you are a leader, success is all about

growing yourself.

When you become a leader, success is all

about growing others."

Jack Welch
Former General Electric CEO and Business ICON

Task Four

The Leadership & Manager Tasks Assessment

Assess Your Capability to Perform 20 Leadership & 40 Management Tasks

Listed below are 60 statements on being a leader and manager. Read each statement and rate your competency level to perform the stated task. Please rate yourself on all 60 statements from one to six. 6 designates you are at the expert level and 1 means you see yourself as incompetent at this time in performing the stated task. The higher your rating, the less coaching and developmental work you see yourself needing to perform the stated task.

Rating Scale

6. Expert –unconsciously competent at performing this task-can coach others
5. Extremely competent at performing this task- no need for coaching
4. Average at performing this task-could use a little coaching at times
3. Somewhat competent at performing this task – would like some steady coaching
2. Not very competent at performing this task- a need for coaching
1. Definitely not competent at performing this task-a strong need for coaching

<u>Team Unit Leader Tasks</u>-We ask you to rate your competency level on the following 20 team unit leadership tasks.

1. I know what my organization/unit looks like today and can work with others to develop a vision of what the organization/unit should become and be at a certain time in the future.

_____6 _____5 _____4 _____3 _____2 _____1

2. I am a strategic thinker and can work with others to develop ongoing strategies to help the organization/unit achieve it's vision and plan.

_____6 _____5 _____4 _____3 _____2 _____1

3. I can create a mission statement with others that can excite, unite and reward every direct report and stakeholder in the organization/unit.

_____6 _____5 _____4 _____3 _____2 _____1

4. I can work with my boss to develop objectives that have the appropriate financial metrics and then assemble a talented team of individuals that will help us achieve our predetermined objectives and turn our vision into reality.

_____6 _____5 _____4 _____3 _____2 _____1

5. I can follow my boss and those who have authority over me as well as lead and delegate responsibilities to those that report to me.

_____6 _____5 _____4 _____3 _____2 _____1

6. I know how to build an implementation network team that is strong and loyal enough to execute our ongoing strategies and plans.

_____6 _____5 _____4 _____3 _____2 _____1

7. I can motivate and inspire people so they have the confidence to overcome any impediments that may prevent them from achieving the established objectives.

_____6 _____5 _____4 _____3 _____2 _____1

8. I know my industry and our market place so I can anticipate and facilitate the changes that our organization/unit needs to make to be successful.

_____6 _____5 _____4 _____3 _____2 _____1

9. I can establish a strong rapport with direct reports so I feel comfortable giving constructive advice and pushing them to meet the challenges (objectives) we set for ourselves.

_____6 _____5 _____4 _____3 _____2 _____1

10. I am a situational leader knowing when I have to be an autocratic or a benevolent dictator and when it is important to be a collaborative and participative leader bringing everyone together to make important decisions. Our financial situation and how much time we have to pull ourselves out of a difficult situation will determine my leadership style.

_____6 _____5 _____4 _____3 _____2 _____1

11. I can get people to listen to me, adopt my ideas and follow me. I read a lot and keep up with what is going on in our organization/unit and industry so when I talk, I persuade people with facts and reasoning and not by just trying to overpower them.

_____6 _____5 _____4 _____3 _____2 _____1

12. I call people by their appropriate name, show warmth, respect and empathy and try to find something we have in common so we can develop a good relationship.

_____6 _____5 _____4 _____3 _____2 _____1

13. I am continually spotting talent in people and encouraging them to use it in their assigned positions and situations. I am always thinking how their talent can be used to help our unit/organization grow.

_____6 _____5 _____4 _____3 _____2 _____1

14. I am a honest, fair and ethical person and instill these values into our organization/unit through modeling behavior.

_____6 _____5 _____4 _____3 _____2 _____1

15. I am genuinely interested in learning about people in the organization as I like to get individuals talking about themselves, their passion, family, concerns and ideas.

_____6 _____5 _____4 _____3 _____2 _____1

16. I like to make people feel important and part of the unit/organization. I write congratulatory letters, give compliments to individuals in a group setting, praise people for their effort and achievements and provide meaningful rewards to those that deserve them.

_____6 _____5 _____4 _____3 _____2 _____1

17. I display enthusiasm and a positive attitude at work and hope this behavior by example will spread throughout our unit/organization.

_____6 _____5 _____4 _____3 _____2 _____1

18. When we have team meetings, I am attentive and show respect for people's ideas so they will continue to share what they know. I believe there is no one as smart as all of us and encourage everyone to share their views, ideas and knowledge. I also encourage team members not to twitter or talk on the phone when someone in the group is talking.

_____6 _____5 _____4 _____3 _____2 _____1

19. I know how to build people's confidence.. If you can't say something worthy about a person, say nothing. You build positive images about people by talking about their strengths and not their weaknesses. You work with people in private meetings to coach them on how to use their strengths and remedy their limitations.

_____6 _____5 _____4 _____3 _____2 _____1

20. I show that I care about each person in my organization/unit. I work with direct reports to set objectives, that if met, will grow their career and the organization/unit.

_____6 _____5 _____4 _____3 _____2 _____1

<u>Management Tasks</u>-We ask you to rate your competency level on the following 40 management tasks.

<u>Rating Scale</u>

6. *Expert- unconsciously competent at performing task*-can coach others
5. *Extremely competent at performing task* - no need for coaching
4. *Average at performing task*-could use a little coaching at times
3. *Somewhat competent at performing task*-would like some steady coaching
2. *Not very competent at performing this task*- a need for coaching
1. *Definitely not competent at performing task*-a strong need for coaching

21. I am experienced and knowledgeable about the steps in the planning process and feel comfortable with the process I use to develop plans.

_____6 _____5 _____4 _____3 _____2 _____1

22. I know how to collect and analyze data and information (competition, changing market place, customer needs and economic factors etc.) so realistic business objectives and plans can be created by me, my boss and direct reports.

_____6 _____5 _____4 _____3 _____2 _____1

23. I can effectively work with my boss to develop business objectives and then meet with my direct reports One on One to review the objectives, solidify them and add others.

_____6 _____5 _____4 _____3 _____2 _____1

24. I can implement the *Gap Analysis and Closure Model* (a methodology used to grow an organization/unit) or a similar planning model. This model helps you identify where you are today in an area (sales of a certain product for example), where you want to be at the end of the year in your sales and the action plans you need to execute to close the gap of where you are today and where you want to be in sales by a certain date tomorrow.

_____6 _____5 _____4 _____3 _____2 _____1

25. I can write clear objectives and teach others how to write good objectives so everyone knows what we need to achieve and when.

_____6 _____5 _____4 _____3 _____2 _____1

26. I can forecast realistic projections of the amount of time, money, manpower and other resources it will take for our organization/unit to achieve its objectives.

_____6 _____5 _____4 _____3 _____2 _____1

27. I know all the chart of accounts that go into developing a budget, what we can allocate and spend in each account and how to make everyone in the organization/unit stay within their budget so we can meet our profit objective.

_____6 _____5 _____4 _____3 _____2 _____1

28. I can read and understand a profit and loss statement, balance sheet and other valuable financial reports that are useful in the planning, monitoring and profit making process.

_____6 _____5 _____4 _____3 _____2 _____1

29. I can help direct reports/individuals develop objectives that will tie into their organization/unit's objectives.

_____6 _____5 _____4 _____3 _____2 _____1

30. I can monitor our plan and make the appropriate changes to make sure our team unit/organization stays on course to meet the objectives. This includes building incentives into the plan so team members are motivated and rewarded throughout the year.

_____6 _____5 _____4 _____3 _____2 _____1

31. I can project the human resource needs of my organization/unit and establish an organizational structure identifying the positions we need to meet our objectives.

_____6 _____5 _____4 _____3 _____2 _____1

32. I can write job descriptions for each position identifying the experience, knowledge and special skills and personality needed by an individual to be successful.

_____6 _____5 _____4 _____3 _____2 _____1

33. I can assess my present direct reports to determine if they meet the qualifications that were established for their position. I am astute enough to know whether I should spend the time developing a direct report or releasing him or her.

34. I can work with our human resource department and recruiters to upgrade the talent in specific positions in my organization/unit.

_____6 _____5 _____4 _____3 _____2 _____1

35. I am effective at interviewing people for specific positions, checking out their references and using assessment instruments to learn about them before an offer is made.

_____6 _____5 _____4 _____3 _____2 _____1

36. I am skilled in process design and improvement, projecting manpower needs, rightsizing and making organizational changes.

_____6 _____5 _____4 _____3 _____2 _____1

37. I have a process that identifies and develops high potential team unit leaders.

_____6 _____5 _____4 _____3 _____2 _____1

38. I have a process that identifies and develops high potential team member leaders.

_____6 _____5 _____4 _____3 _____2 _____1

39. I can execute a leadership and performance management system (organization effectiveness model) that transforms all direct reports into champion performers and my organization/ unit into a championship organization.

_____6 _____5 _____4 _____3 _____2 _____1

40. I possess good time management and organization skills and use the appropriate technology to get more work done than the average team unit leader/manager.

_____6 _____5 _____4 _____3 _____2 _____1

41. I can operate as an effective One on One Idiosyncratic Manager (knowing an individual so well that you can help him grow and perform at a high level) and bring out the best in each direct report.

_____6 _____5 _____4 _____3 _____2 _____1

42. I know the assessment instruments/materials to use to learn about my direct reports. (what motivates and de-motivates them, their career interests, skills, values, needs, desire to be a team unit leader or team member leader and career aspiration).

_____6 _____5 _____4 _____3 _____2 _____1

43. I am very effective at meeting with direct reports One on One to gain their support on the team unit objectives that my boss and I want to achieve. I am also skillful at obtaining their ideas on other growth objectives that will make our unit/organization better.

_____6 _____5 _____4 _____3 _____2 _____1

44. I can work One on One with each direct report and teach them the business planning and the Gap Analysis and Closure Model that we will use to develop our plan.

_____6 _____5 _____4 _____3 _____2 _____1

45. I am effective at sitting down with each of my direct reports One on One and helping them develop their growth (champion building) objectives for the year. Each direct report's objectives will tie into achieving the team unit's growth objectives which includes growing team members as well as the unit.

_____6 _____5 _____4 _____3 _____2 _____1

46. I am effective at meeting with my direct reports One on One monthly to monitor and track their progress and make adjustments so the personal and the team unit's business objectives are met.

_____6 _____5 _____4 _____3 _____2 _____1

47. I am effective at meeting with my direct reports One on One to maintain harmony and good working relationships between team members. If dissonance is occurring between me and a direct report or between two direct reports, we will solve the issue One on One and not in a team meeting where it makes problems more difficult to solve.

_____6 _____5 _____4 _____3 _____2 _____1

48. I can meet with direct reports One on One and identify the tasks they must perform to be the best in their field. I will identify each task and help them move from an unwilling and unable state to an expert (able and willing) position.

49 I can work One on One with each direct report and teach them how to manage and take charge of their career journey.

_____6 _____5 _____4 _____3 _____2 _____1

50. I can work One on One with each direct report and help them become an effective team unit and team member leader. I will suggest they take the Mulligan Leadership Analysis Survey, review their results and develop a leadership growth plan for both roles.

_____6 _____5 _____4 _____3 _____2 _____1

51. I can collaborate with direct reports and decide on the objectives we must meet to transform ourselves into a championship or high performing unit/organization.

_____6 _____5 _____4 _____3 _____2 _____1

52. I know what assessment tools to use to learn about the group dynamics of our unit and have a process that will build team cohesiveness and keep the team moving forward to meet it's objectives..

_____6 _____5 _____4 _____3 _____2 _____1

53. I can establish a monthly and quarterly metric/ monitoring system to keep the team members informed on how they and the team unit are doing in achieving their predetermined objectives.

_____6 _____5 _____4 _____3 _____2 _____1

54. I can conduct monthly motivational meetings so every team member keeps their enthusiasm about transforming themselves and the team unit into the best in the field or class.

_____6 _____5 _____4 _____3 _____2 _____1

55. I can create a think tank environment where direct reports are rewarded for ideas that help the unit/organization become more streamlined, competitive and profitable.

_____6 _____5 _____4 _____3 _____2 _____1

56. I am familiar with the literature on what satisfies and dissatisfies people at work. I have a work satisfaction survey I use to learn about my direct reports satisfaction with work and use the information to improve the work and team environment.

_____6 _____5 _____4 _____3 _____2 _____1

57. I know how to use the normative group process with direct reports to discover what they view as the major impediments to achieving each unit objective. This process is also used to gain their ideas on how to overcome these impediments to achieve each objective.

_____6 _____5 _____4 _____3 _____2 _____1

58. I am very familiar with the theories on Self Actualization. I know a survey I can use that will tell me if the needs of my direct reports are being met. I know if the security, safety and social needs of my direct reports aren't being met, they will not be able to focus on their job and become the best at what we ask them to do.

_____6 _____5 _____4 _____3 _____2 _____1

59. I can create a helping and performance facilitation work environment with all my direct reports by putting them through a special team achievement program and communication training program.

_____6 _____5 _____4 _____3 _____2 _____1

60. I can help the team unit develop an ongoing team unit resume of accomplishments so each team member sees what the unit has accomplished each month and for the year. This builds confidence and unity and help team members build stronger resumes. We can then wave our flag in the organization so we are noticed for our fine work.

_____6 _____5 _____4 _____3 _____2 _____1

Calculate Your Scores for 20 Leadership and 40 Management Tasks

Listed below are *two leadership and four management functions*. There are 10 statements on the survey for each of the six functions. Review each statement on the survey and if you scored a 6, place 15 points by the phrase number below; if your scored a 5, place 12 points by the phrase number below; if you scored a 4, place 9 points on the phrase number below; if you scored a 3, place 6 points on the phrase number below; if you scored a 2, place 3 points by the phrase number below and if you scored a 1, place 0 points by the phrase number below. Then add up all the points to learn your total score for that particular function. The score range is 0 to 150. Place your total score for each function on the following page and learn the level where you perceive yourself functioning at this time.

(Two Leadership Functions)
Executing Leadership Tasks
(Assess Where You Are Today and Identify Where You Need to be Tomorrow)

1___ 2___ 3___ 4___ 5___ 6___ 7___ 8___ 9___ 10___
Total Points_____

Executing Tasks to Build Your Personal Power
(You Want People to Like, Believe in and Follow You)

11___ 12___ 13___ 14___ 15___ 16___ 17___ 18___ 19___ 20___
Total Points_____

(Five Management Functions)
Executing Tasks to Develop a Vision and Growth Plan for Your Unit/Organization
(Identify Where You Are Today and Create a Vision and Growth Plan that will Take You Where You Want the Organization to be Next Year at this Time)

21___ 22___ 23___ 24___ 25___ 26___ 27___ 28___ 29___ 30___
Total Points_____

Executing Tasks that Provides You with the Right Organization and Talent to Make Plan
(You need to identify your human resource needs and then find the talent to make Plan)

31___ 32___ 33___ 34___ 35___ 36___ 37___ 38___ 39___ 40___
Total Points_____

Executing Tasks that Helps You Build an Effective One on One System to Make Plan
(You manage, motivate and monitor people's progress in One on One sessions to make Plan)

41___ 42___ 43___ 44___ 45___ 46___ 47___ 48___ 49___ 50___
Total Points_____

Executing Tasks that Helps You Build Team Cohesiveness and Team Play to Make Plan

(You bring everyone together as a team and reinforce team play to make Plan)

 51____ 52____ 53____ 54____ 55____ 56____ 57____ 58____ 59____ 60____

Total Points_____

Copyright © 2018 Michael V. Mulligan

67

<u>Review Your Leadership and Management</u>
<u>Capability Scores and Functioning Levels</u>

We have combined your 60 answers into two leadership and four management areas. Your total points, which should be recorded in the right column below, will place you on one of five levels. The higher your score and level, the more you perceive yourself as capable of performing the 10 tasks under each area.. The lower your score and level, the less likely you see yourself executing the 10 tasks under the leadership or management areas. <u>Keep in mind that this profile represents the perceptions you have of yourself and is not a test.</u> The score range is 0 to 150.

If you fall at level 5 or at Level 4 with a score of 90 and above, you view yourself as capable of handling most of the 10 tasks included in that one area.. If your score is 60 to 90 and fall at a 3 level, you see yourself as average in carrying out the 10 tasks under the function. If you fall at Level 2 or 1 with a score of 60 or less, you view yourself somewhat opposite of the function or area being described. This information can help you be an effective team unit leader & team member leader.

	150	120	90	60	30	0
Six Areas	**Definitely Like You Scores of 120 to 150**	**Usually Like You Scores of 90 to 119**	**Somewhat Like You Scores of 60 to 89**	**A Little Like You Scores of 30 to 59**	**Not Like You Scores of 0 to 29**	**Scores**
<u>Leadership</u> **Leading Direct Reports**	Level 5	Level 4	Level 3	Level 2	Level 1	
Building My Personal Power with Direct Reports	Level 5	Level 4	Level 3	Level 2	Level 1	
<u>Management</u> **Developing a Plan**	Level 5	Level 4	Level 3	Level 2	Level 1	
Organizing and Hiring Talent	Level 5	Level 4	Level 3	Level 2	Level 1	
One on One Management	Level 5	Level 4	Level 3	Level 2	Level 1	
Building Team Cohesiveness and Team Play	Level 5	Level 4	Level 3	Level 2	Level 1	

Task Five

Evaluate Your Management Skills

Evaluate yourself on the provided lines that reflect your skill level at this time. If you have not had a lot of work experience, rate yourself in regard to group activities and leadership experience.

5	Excellent Skills	(No Developmental Need)
4	Above Average Skills	(Minimum Developmental Need)
3	Average Skills	(Moderate Developmental Need)
2	Below Average Skills	(Above-Average Developmental Need)
1	Poor Skills	(Strong Developmental Need)

There are ten skill categories. Under each category, add up your points and divide by the total number of items to obtain an average. Finally, rank-order your mean scores by category to learn which management areas you need coaching and should work on the most.

Category 1: Self Management:

1) Able to compete in an objective-oriented environment. _____
2) Able to establish individual objectives, plans of action and your own work structure. _____
3) Able to accept the goals and objectives of others and work toward accomplishing them. _____
4) Able to handle pressure and stressful situations without losing composure and objectivity. _____
5) Able to set priorities and manage time effectively. _____
6) Able to be assertive and aggressive when necessary. _____
7) Able to make decisions. _____
8) Able to display a high level of self-discipline. _____
9) Able to relate to people at work. _____
10) Able to analyze and solve problems. _____
11) Able to achieve stated objectives through persistence. _____
12) Able to work independently or as a member of a team. _____
13) Able to be both a leader and a follower. _____
14) Able to be confident and in charge of your own destiny. _____

Total Points_____/14 = Average = [   ]

Category 2: Planning:

1) Able to help the company, division and department establish objectives.

2) Able to use the GAP Analysis Model – establishing and achieving objectives and creation action tasks to close the gap.

3) Able to assess where my group is today in relation to predetermined objectives

4) Able to forecast realistic projections of the amount of time, money and manpower it will take to reach my objectives.

5) Able to establish budgets, stay within the budget and control spending.

6) Able to determine and write policies and procedures.

7) Able to develop in writing a plan of action or a program.

8) Able to be flexible and modify plans when the need arises — controlling change.

9) Able to communicate plans both in writing and orally.

Total Points =	
Total Points _____ / 9 = Average =	

Category 3: Organizing and Staffing:

1) Able to establish an organizational structure and a chart delineating relationships.

2) Able to create and write job descriptions.

3) Able to project manpower needs.

4) Able to develop succession planning in the company (training someone to take the place of someone else).

5) Able to recruit high potential and talented people.

6) Able to interview well so I can determine the right person for the position.

7) Able to select a staff that can perform, work together and achieve stated objectives.

8) Able to orient people so they understand the company's objectives, their job responsibilities and what is expected of them.

9)   Able to assess training needs, establish training programs and train staff.

10) Able to help people with their career development.

Total Points =	
Total Points _____ **/ 10 = Average =**	

Category 4: Supervising and Directing:

1)   Able to get people to establish objectives and a work plan compatible to the division and department.

2)   Able to decide what work activities you should do and what tasks you should delegate.

3)   Able to use a Coaching Model – identifying the areas where one needs coaching or to be empowered.

4)   Able to understand individuals, what motivates them and be able to apply that knowledge.

5)   Able to coordinate the efforts and gain the cooperation of people to work together toward a common goal.

6)   Able to reward and reprimand people in a timely fashion.

7)   Able to conduct productive group meetings.

8)   Able to manage individuals through face-to-face meetings.

9)   Able to develop good interpersonal relationships with staff and colleagues.

10) Able to persuade and sell people on your ideas.

11) Able to develop performance standards.

12) Able to establish a reporting system.

13) Able to measure results.

14) Able to conduct a performance appraisal.

15) Able to empower individuals to perform specific tasks.

Total Points =	
Total Points _____ **/ 15 = Average =**	

Category 5: Operations and Research:

1) Able to perform research and development activities: basic R&D, applied R&D, production engineering, design, testing and follow-up. _____

2) Able to perform production activities: plant engineer, industrial engineering, purchasing, production planning and control, manufacturing and quality control. _____

3) Able to perform marketing activities: marketing research, advertising, sales planning, sales promotion, sales operation and physical distribution. _____

4) Able to perform financial activities: financial planning and relations, tax management, custody of funds, credit and collection and insurance. _____

5) Able to control: general accounting, cost accounting, budget planning and control, internal auditing, systems and procedures. _____

6) Able to do personnel administration work: employment, wage and salary administration, industrial relations, organization planning and development. _____

7) Able to promote external relations: public relations, credits and investor communication, civic affairs, association and community relations. _____

8) Able to handle legal and corporate relations: corporate legal matters, patents, employee legal questions, stockholder relations, board of director activities and corporate affairs. _____

	Total Points =
Total Points _____ / 8 = Average =	

Category 6: Clerical and Administrative

1) Able to use computers and various software. _____

2) Able to use e-mail, voice mail, fax machines and latest technology _____

3) Able to establish a filing system. _____

4) Able to handle budgets and billing. _____

1) Able to organize yourself and your office area. _____
2) Able to coordinate supply inventory. _____
3) Able to send out invoices and collect payments. _____
4) Able to pay invoices and balance checkbook. _____

	Total Points
Total Points _____ / 8 = Average =	

Category 7: Construction and Trades:

1) Able to draft. _____
2) Able to do mechanical tasks. _____
3) Able to build (carpentry). _____
4) Able to do electrical work. _____
5) Able to repair things. _____
6) Able to comprehend and solve technical problems _____

	Total Points
Total Points _____ / 6 = Average =	

Category 8: Entertaining/ Performing-Skills to gain you visibility

1) Able to write creatively: articles, poems, books, plays, etc. _____
2) Able to speak in front of groups. _____
3) Able to dance. _____
4) Able to sing. _____
5) Athletic ability. _____
6) Able to act. _____
7) Able to organize productions. _____

	Total Points
Total Points _____ / 7 = Average =	

Category 9: Sales and Marketing

1) Able to analyze the needs of my marketplace. _____
2) Able to develop a marketing strategy. _____
3) Able to calculate market share. _____
4) Able to do sales calls, to meet and relate to a variety of people. _____
5) Able to learn about your products and services. _____
6) Able to deal with rejection. _____
7) Able to ask for the order, be persistent and obtain it. _____
8) Able to tolerate and be patient with people. _____
9) Able to develop a sales plan. _____
10) Able to be a needs assessment salesperson instead of selling everything you have until something sticks. _____

	Total Points	
Total Points _____ / 10 = Average =		

Category 10: Interpersonal Relationships

1) Able to communicate with empathy. _____
2) Able to communicate warmth and a caring attitude. _____
3) Able to listen and hear what the person is really saying. _____
4) Able to communicate respect for the individual. _____
5) Able to focus on the interests of others. _____
6) Able to confront someone when they are not walking the talk _____
7) Able to respond and help people understand their situations more clearly so they can solve their own problems. _____

	Total Points	
Total Points _____ / 7 = Average		

Below, rank yourself in the ten skill areas in order of points.

1._____ Self-Management   2._____ Planning
3._____ Organizing and Staffing 4._____ Supervising and Directing
5._____ Operations and Research 6._____ Clerical
7._____ Construction and Trades 8._____ Entertaining and Performing
9._____ Sales and Marketing   10._____ Interpersonal Relationships

Where do you need to make improvement?

Task Six

Analyze Your Personal and Work Values

Below is a list of values and their definitions. Review this list and use the definitions listed to rate your values on the following page. When we occupy a team unit role or team member role, our value system is always at work. If we do not honor or live the values that are most important to us, we need to evaluate what we are doing or not doing and make changes so we can live within ourselves.

1. **ACHIEVEMENT** - Accomplishment; a result brought about by resolve, persistence, or endeavor. The work "achieve" is defined as "to bring to a successful conclusion; accomplishment or to attain a desired end or aim."

2. **ALTRUISM** - Regard for or devotion to the interests of others.

3. **AUTONOMY** - The ability to be a self-determining individual.

4. **CREATIVITY** - The creating of new and innovative ideas and designs.

5. **EMOTIONAL WELL-BEING** - Freedom from overwhelming anxieties and barriers to effective functioning; a peace of mind; inner security.

6. **HEALTH** - The condition of being sound in body; freedom from physical disease or pain; the general condition of the body; well-being.

7. **HONESTY** - Fairness or straightforwardness of conduct; integrity; uprightness of character or action and authentic (not a pretender)

8. **JUSTICE** - The quality of being impartial or fair; righteousness; conformity to truth, fact, or reason; to treat others fairly or adequately.

9. **KNOWLEDGE** - The seeking of truth, information or principles for the satisfaction of curiosity, for use, or for the power of knowing.

10. **LOVE** - Affection based on admiration or benevolence; warm attachment, enthusiasm, or devotion; unselfish devotion that freely accepts another in loyalty and seeks his good.

11. **LOYALTY** – Maintaining allegiance to a person, group, institution, or political entity.

12. **MORALITY** – The belief in and keeping of ethical standards.

13. **PHYSICAL APPEARANCE** – Concern for the beauty and looks of one's own body.

14. **PLEASURE** – The agreeable emotion accompanying the possession or expectation of what is good or greatly desired. "Pleasure" stresses satisfaction or gratification rather than visible happiness; a state of gratification.

15. **POWER** – Possession of control, authority, or influence over others.

16. **RECOGNITION** – Being made to feel significant and important; being given special notice or attention by others

17. **RELIGIOUS FAITH** – Communion with, obedience to and activity on behalf of a Supreme Being.

18. **SKILL** – The ability to use one's knowledge, technical expertise and physical attributes effectively and readily in execution of performance;

19. TRUST – Knowing that you have the backing of a person and he/she is on your side.

20. WEALTH – Abundance of valuable material possessions or resources; affluence.

21. WISDOM – The ability to discern inner qualities and relationships; insight, good sense, judgment and make wise decisions

RATE YOUR PERSONAL VALUES

Each of the groups below contains five values. In the parenthesis preceding each value, place a number from 1 to 5. Number 5 represents your HIGHEST ranking value in that group; number 1 represents the value you rank the LOWEST in that group. Be sure to number each value, and you must give a different rating to each value listed in that group of five. Repeat the same process 21 times below.

1   [] Achievement
    [] Altruism
    [] Justice
    [] Religious Faith
    [] Wealth

2   [] Altruism
    [] Autonomy
    [] Loyalty
    [] Power
    [] Recognition

3   [] Creativity
    [] Love
    [] Pleasure
    [] Recognition
    [] Wealth

4   [] Trust
    [] Justice
    [] Pleasure
    [] Power
    [] Wisdom

5   [] Altruism
    [] Honesty
    [] Love
    [] Physical
    Appearance
    [] Wisdom

8   [] Autonomy
    [] Emotional Well Being
    [] Health
    [] Wealth
    [] Wisdom

9   [] Honesty
    [] Knowledge
    [] Power
    [] Skill
    [] Wealth

10 [] Achievement
    [] Emotional Well-being
    [] Love
    [] Morality
    [] Power

11 [] Trust
    [] Autonomy
    [] Knowledge
    [] Love
    [] Religious Faith

12 [] Trust
    [] Loyalty
    [] Morality
    [] Physical Appearance

    [] Wealth

15 [] Trust
    [] Altruism
    [] Creativity
    [] Emotional Well-being
    [] Skill

16 [] Emotional Well-being
    [] Justice
    [] Knowledge
    [] Physical Appearance
    [] Recognition 37

17 [] Altruism
    [] Health
    [] Knowledge
    [] Morality
    [] Pleasure

18 [] Morality
    [] Recognition
    [] Religious Faith
    [] Skill
    [] Wisdom

19 [] Emotional Well-Being
    [] Honesty
    [] Loyalty
    [] Pleasure

    [] Religious Faith

78

6	[] Achievement	13	[] Creativity	20	[] Achievement
	[] Trust		[] Health		[] Creativity
	[] Health		[] Physical Appearance		[] Knowledge
	[] Honesty		[] Power		[] Loyalty
	[] Recognition		[] Religious Faith		[] Wisdom

7	[] Achievement	14	[] Health	21	[] Autonomy
	[] Autonomy		[] Justice		[] Creativity
	[] Physical Appearance		[] Love		[] Honesty
	[] Pleasure		[] Loyalty		[] Justice
	[] Skill		[] Skill		[] Moralit

(Score and Rank Values On Next Page)

1. **ACHIEVEMENT –**
   1_____
   6_____
   7_____
   10 _____
   20 _____
   Total_____

2. **ALTRUISM –**
   1_____
   2_____
   5_____
   15_____
   17_____
   Total_____

3. **AUTONOMY –**
   2_____
   7_____
   8_____
   11_____
   21_____
   Total_____

8. **JUSTICE –**
   1_____
   4_____
   14_____
   16_____
   21_____
   Total_____

9. **KNOWLEDGE –**
   9_____
   11_____
   16_____
   17_____
   20_____
   Total_____

10. **LOVE –**
   3_____
   5_____
   10_____
   11_____
   14_____
   Total_____

15. **POWER –**
   2_____
   4_____
   9_____
   10_____
   13_____
   Total_____

16. **RECOGNITION**
   – 2_____
   3_____
   6_____
   16_____
   18_____
   Total _____

17. **RELIGIOUS FAITH**
   1 _____
   11 _____
   13 _____
   18 _____
   19 _____
   Total_____

4. CREATIVITY –

3_____

13_____

15_____

20_____

21_____

Total_____

5. EMOTIONAL WELL-BEING –

8_____

10_____

15_____

16_____

19_____

Total_____

6. HEALTH –

6_____

8_____

13_____

14_____

17_____

Total_____

7. HONESTY -

5_____

6_____

9_____

19_____

21 _____

Total _____

11. LOYALTY –

2_____

12_____

14_____

19_____

20_____

Total_____

12. MORALITY –

10_____

12_____

17_____

18_____

21_____

Total_____

13. PHYSICAL APPEARANCE –

5_____

7_____

12_____

13_____

16_____

Total_____

14. PLEASURE –

3_____

4_____

7_____

17_____

19_____

Total _____

18. SKILL –

7_____

9_____

14_____

15_____

18_____

Total_____

19. TRUST –

4_____

6_____

11_____

12_____

15_____

Total_____

20. WEALTH –

1_____

3_____

8_____

9_____

12_____

Total_____

21. WISDOM –

4_____

5_____

8_____

18_____

20 _____

Total_____

CALCULATE YOUR SCORES AND RANK YOUR VALUES

LIST YOUR TOP FIVE VALUES- INCLUDES VALUES WITH HIGHEST SCORES

List Your Bottom Five Values-Lowest Scores

WERE YOU SURPRISED AT YOUR RESULTS? IF SO WHY?

ARE YOU HONORING AND LIVING YOUR TOP FIVE VALUES?

Take Work Values Survey and Rank What You Want Most from Work

To examine your values, please review the 30 values listed below in relation to their level of importance to you at this time (1 being the <u>LEAST important</u> and 5 being <u>EXTREMELY important</u>) and circle the corresponding numb*er*.

VALUES IN LIFE AND WORK	Least	Somewhat	Moderate	High	Extreme
1. Making my own decisions.	1	2	3	4	5
2. Loyalty at work.	1	2	3	4	5
3. Being content with my work.	1	2	3	4	5
4. Being well liked.	1	2	3	4	5
5. Challenging myself intellectually.	1	2	3	4	5
6. Having low work stress.	1	2	3	4	5
7. Advancing my career.	1	2	3	4	5
8. Being independent.	1	2	3	4	5
9. Helping society.	1	2	3	4	5
10. Freedom of time/controlling work schedule.	1	2	3	4	5
11. Using new skills and knowledge.	1	2	3	4	5
12. Maintaining physical fitness.	1	2	3	4	5
13. Choosing my own work location.	1	2	3	4	5
14. Being well known.	1	2	3	4	5
15. Working primarily alone.	1	2	3	4	5
16. Spending time with friends and family.	1	2	3	4	5
17. Serving others.	1	2	3	4	5
18. Being creative.	1	2	3	4	5
19. Being self-motivated.	1	2	3	4	5
20. Being active in the community.	1	2	3	4	5
21. Participating in competitive situations.	1	2	3	4	5
22. Collaborating with colleagues.	1	2	3	4	5

23.	Having power and authority.	1	2	3	4	5
24.	Having a high income.	1	2	3	4	5
25.	Being part of a team.	1	2	3	4	5
26.	Having job security.	1	2	3	4	5
27.	Having status.	1	2	3	4	5
28.	Having major accomplishments.	1	2	3	4	5
29.	Influencing others.	1	2	3	4	5
30.	Pursuing excellence.	1	2	3	4	5

Summary of Values

List the scores below that you had for each of the 30 values and total them:

	Question	List The # For Your Answer
ACHIEVEMENT: **A Sense Of Accomplishment By Doing Challenging Tasks. Becoming The Best**	5	
	11	
	18	
	21	
	28	
	30	
	Total Score	
AFFILIATION: **A Sense Of Belonging; Feeling A Part Of The Group. Working In A Collaborative Work Environment.**	2	
	4	
	9	
	17	
	22	
	25	
	Total Score	
STATUS-ACQUIRING: **Moving Up And Having More Symbols Of Success. Obtaining Titles And More Compensation.**	7	
	14	
	23	
	24	
	27	
	29	
	Total Score	
ENTERPRISING: **A Feeling Of Being In Charge; Self-Management; Working Independently. Being Accountable For My Plan Of Action.**	1	
	8	
	10	
	13	
	15	
	19	
	Total Score	

Balance Of Life/Stabilized Lifestyle:	3
	6
Continuity At Work And Having Time For	12
Commitments Outside Of Work. Knowing	16
There Is Something Else Out There Rather	20
Than Work.	26
	Total Score

Please rank your five value areas by the total scores:

1._____   2._____   3._____   4._____   5._____

Complete the Work Rewards Survey and Determine if You are Obtaining What You Want Most from Work

This exercise is designed to help you examine your work rewards. You cannot set a career goal without understanding what is most important to your work life. Therefore, carefully think through this exercise and review the 25 areas listed below. Rank the 25 rewards 1 through 25 with 1 being of <u>high importance</u> and 25 being of <u>lower importance</u>. Circle your top five work rewards. Are your top five work rewards being met at this time or will they be met in the future?

_____   1.   Authority and responsibility: How much position power does the company give me?

_____   2.   Compensation package: Salary, bonus, insurance, stock options, car, country club, etc.

_____   3.   Location: What is the commuting time? In what part of the country is the job located?

_____   4.   Independence: How much will I be supervised? Can I work from home?

_____   5.   Team orientation: A team atmosphere in which people work closely together.

_____   6.   Type of industry: Is the company in a growth industry?

_____   7.   Professional growth: Does the company offer training & pay for continuing education?

_____   8.   Travel: How much time will I be on the road?

_____   9.   Time: How much time will I spend on various work tasks?

_____   10.   Flexibility: How many hours per week will I work? Can I alter my work schedule to meet my family situation? Can I work from home?

_____   11.   Supervisor: Can I learn from him/her? What is his or her management style?

_____   12.   Work environment/culture: Formal or more laid back? Progressive or conservative?

_____   13.   Personality chemistry: Does my personality fit in with most of the personalities of the people in my department/office/firm?

_____   14.   Physical labor vs. mental work: Will I be using my mind or doing things physically?

_____ 15. Opportunity for advancement: Does the company have a career advancement program?

_____ 16. A chance to help others.

_____ 17. Accumulating wealth.

_____ 18. Becoming an expert or best in my field.

_____ 19. Receiving recognition for my work.

_____ 20. Having time for leisure.

_____ 21. Being able to work creatively.

_____ 22. Having daily contact with people.

_____ 23. Offering a day care center for my children

_____ 24. Being in a fast-paced environment with other competitive people.

_____ 25. Having job security in my present position.

TASK SEVEN

EVALUATE YOUR PERSONAL AND SOCIAL MATURITY-(E.Q.

Please Rate Yourself on This Human Relations Maturity Survey

Please rate yourself on the following 30 statements. Evaluate yourself on a scale of 0 to 6, with 6 representing <u>definitely like you</u> and 0 representing <u>definitely</u> <u>not like you</u>.

_____ 1.　I am aware of my interests, skills, experiences, talent, values, and leadership ability.

_____ 2.　I never let things or others upset me so much that I blow up or lose my cool.

_____ 3.　I am aware of what motivates me and de-motivates me.

_____ 4.　I am very effective at identifying the feelings of others and stating the feeling words back to that person showing empathy.

_____ 5.　I have the ability to listen and influence others.

_____ 6.　I am aware of my limitations and know what I need to work on to develop each into strengths.

_____ 7.　I am aware of my obsessions and know when I become overly compulsive.

_____ 8.　I am constantly striving to improve and meet my own standard of excellence.

_____ 9.　I am very sensitive to other people's feelings and I am a caring person.

_____ 10.　I can negotiate and resolve disagreements.

_____ 11.　I am aware of my emotions and know what causes me to be in these different states.

_____ 12.　I can establish my own objectives, plan of action and work structure.

_____ 13.　I am committed to pursuing the growth goals and achieving the objectives of my team, organization and college/university.

_____ 14.　I can help others identify their developmental needs and bolster their confidence to be the best they can be.

_____ 15.　I have the ability to inspire and lead individuals and groups.

_____ 16.　I have a strong sense of self worth and know I am capable of being the best I can be.

_____ 17.　I take responsibility for my own actions and personal performance.

Human Relations Maturity Survey Continued

_____ 18. I am always ready and alert to act on opportunities that make me, my team and organization better.

_____ 19. I can anticipate, recognize and meet the needs of others.

_____ 20. I have the ability to initiate and manage change.

_____ 21. I know when I say something that offends others.

_____ 22. I am very flexible and adaptable.

_____ 23. I am always optimistic and look at the glass as half full instead of half empty.

_____ 24. I realize that you can cultivate opportunities and success through people who have different experiences, backgrounds and come from different cultures.

_____ 25. I am extremely effective at creating group synergy and pursuing collective goals.

_____ 26. I know what career positions would be best for me at this time.

_____ 27. I am very comfortable with novel ideas, approaches and new information

_____ 28. I have a high want and high will to win.

_____ 29. I am politically astute, being able to read the group's emotional currents and power relationships.

_____ 30. I am extremely effective at creating group synergy and pursuing collective goals.

Please place your answers (numbers) on the following pages to determine your Emotional Intelligence score.

Determining Your Human Relations Maturity or E.Q. Score

Daniel Goldman defines emotional intelligence as "managing feelings so that they are expressed appropriately and effectively, enabling people to work together to accomplish their common goals." Dr. Goldman breaks emotional intelligence into *five competencies*. *Three* competencies are categorized under *Personal Competence* and the other *two* are placed under *Social Competence*.

Personal Competence
(Three categories)

1) Self Awareness
- Emotional awareness
- Accurate self assessment
- Self confidence

1. _____ 6. _____ 11. _____ 16. _____ 21. _____ 26. _____

Total Score:_____ (write your scores down for each of the survey items and add them up)

2) Self Regulation
- Self control
- Trustworthiness
- Conscientiousness
- Adaptability
- Innovation

2. _____ 7. _____ 12. _____ 17. _____ 22. _____ 27. _____

Total Score:_____ (write your scores down for each of the survey items and add them up)

3) **Motivation**

- Achievement driven
- Committed
- Initiative
- Optimistic

3. _____ 8. _____ 13. _____ 18. _____ 23. _____ 28. _____

Total Score:_____ (write your scores down for each of the survey items and add them up)

<u>**Social Competence**</u>
(Two categories)

1) <u>Empathy</u>
- Understanding other people's feelings
- Developing others
- Service orientation
- Leveraging diversity
- Political awareness

4. _____ 9. _____ 14. _____ 19. _____ 24. _____ 29. _____

Total Score:_____ (write your scores down for each of the survey items and add them up)

2) <u>Social Skills</u>
- Influence
- Communication
- Conflict management
- Leadership
- Change catalyst
- Building bonds
- Collaboration and cooperation
- Team capabilities

5. _____ 10. _____ 15. _____ 20. _____ 25. _____ 30. _____

Total Score:_____ (write your scores down for each of the survey items and add them up)

<u>**Total Emotional Intelligence Maturity Score**</u>

Self Awareness	_____		Scoring:	
Self Regulation	_____	180-150	Extremely mature	
Motivation	_____	149-120	Above average maturity	
Empathy	_____	119-90	Average maturity	
Social Skills	_____	89-60	Below average	
		59-0	Extremely immature	

TOTAL SCORE _____

Scores range are from 0 to 36 on each of the five competencies. A score of 25 and above gives you a grade of 70% which would be passing but you might want to raise your score with an improvement plan.

Goldman's Research on Emotional Intelligence

Daniel Goldman, in his book: *Working with Emotional Intelligence*, discussed three areas that make us successful on the job. They are:

- I.Q. – our ability to comprehend and learn things quickly
- Technical expertise and experience
- Emotional intelligence

Goldman discovered that emotional intelligence had to do more with emerging as a leader and becoming a star performer than I.Q. and technical expertise.

David McClelland found that outstanding performers were not just strong in initiative or influence but had strengths across the board, which included the five emotional intelligence areas: self-awareness, self-regulation, motivation, empathy and social skills.

McClelland discovered that the emotional competencies that most often led to star status were:

- Initiative, achievement, drive and adaptability
- Influence, team leadership and political awareness
- Empathy, self-confidence and developing others

The two most common traits that prevented people from becoming star performers were:

- Rigidity: These individuals were unable to adapt their style to changes in the organizational culture or to be flexible or to respond to feedback about traits they needed to change or improve. They couldn't listen or learn.

- Poor Relationships: This was the most single frequently mentioned factor. Individuals were being too harshly critical, insensitive or demanding and this alienated those that work for and with that person.

Daniel Goldman conducted research using his competence model with 181 different job positions in 121 companies worldwide. The model asked management to profile excellence for each job. Emotional competence mattered twice as much as I.Q. and expertise. Since 1918, the average I.Q. score in the United States has risen 24 points. Goldman says that as people have grown smarter in I.Q., their emotional intelligence has declined.

Task Eight

Analyze Your Present Performance Management System

Discuss Your Performance Management Model and its Success

A team performance management model is a process that team unit leaders use to establish team objectives and work with and through each direct report to achieve the objectives. A performance management model should include a cause or mission statement that motivates direct reports to achieve the objectives. The success of any team leader not only depends on the model but other factors such as:

- Having the right people in place and gaining their support.
- The level of difficulty of the growth objectives and the time lines you have to achieve the objectives.
- Whether you and your staff believe the objectives are achievable.
- The level of authority or position power you have to achieve the objectives.
- Having the budget and necessary resources to meet the objectives.
- Believing the company has the best products and service in the industry.
- The unknowns in the market place.
- Having an excellent working relationship with your boss, direct reports, and the employees who you need to support unit in meeting its objectives.

A team unit leader has to establish a performance management model that helps his/her unit, division and the company meet their growth objectives. This accomplishment should increase the value of the company stock, and transform direct reports into expert leaders/ champion performers and the team units, divisions and the company into the best in their fields. A win-win performance management system will give everyone in the company a chance to be rewarded financially, grow and advance their career. An effective performance management model will provide team unit leaders with a process they can use through out their career journey to advance their unit and career.

Rate Your Performance Management Model as It is Today. Rate its Success?
Use the scale 0 to 10.
0=Poor - 10=Extremely Effective. Your Rating Score_____

Analyzing Your Present Performance Management Model

Briefly describe how your company, division, and department work together to establish their vision and mission statements, growth objectives ..

Briefly describe how meeting the growth objectives are monitored.

Briefly describe what motivates employees to achieve the objectives of the company, division and department.

How would you rate your present model on a scale of 0 to 10 with 10 being excellent and 0 being bad?

What would you change in your Model to make it better today?

Would you consider using the **Triangle Team leadership Model?**

Analyzing Your Leadership Strengths / Weaknesses and Making Improvements

Identify where you are on the Management Ladder today and where you would like to be in five years. (Put an X by your present management position and a Y by where you want to be)

_____CEO   _____President   _____Chief Level Officer

_____Senior Vice President   _____Vice President   _____Director

_____Manager   _____Supervisor   _____Project Manager

After assessing yourself, list the areas below where you need to improve.

The 22 Leadership Behaviors- List the areas that need to be improved.

The Mulligan Leadership Personality Profile- Which of the eight behaviors do you need to improve?

Performing 20 Leadership and 40 Management Tasks –Which leadership and management skills do you need to improve?
(Leadership Tasks)

(Management Tasks)

Management Skills- 10 Areas- List the areas you need to improve

<u>Personal Values –</u> What were your five highest personal values and are they being honored in your present position?

Work Values- How did your results turn out? What was the ranking of the five values below?

_____Achievement

_____Affiliation

_____Status/ Acquiring

_____Entrepreneur

_____ Balance of Life

Work Rewards- Of the 25, what were your top five?

E.Q.- Social and Personal Maturity- Which of the five E.Q. areas do you need to improve?

_____ Self Awareness

_____Self Regulation

_____ Motivation

_____Empathy

_____Social Skills

How did you rate your organizations performance management model? What do you need to do to improve your Model?

John Wooden, a hall of fame basketball coach who led the UCLA Bruins to ten National College Basketball Championships was written up in *Sports Illustrated* years ago and under his picture, the caption read,

"The guy who puts the ball through the hoop has ten hands. The strong winds of resistance facing many teams are the players themselves".

The first factor is the personality and the diversity make-up of the team.

The **second factor** is how each player reacts to each other.

A **third** and extremely important factor is attitude. If you can work and perform as a team, your chances for being successful in life and a career will improve.

Section Three-

Review the *TEAM* Program

Task # One-

Assess How You Lead and Behave In a Group

(LEADING A TEAM OR GROUP MEETING)

READ THE FOLLOWING 20 STATEMENTS AND RATE YOUR SELF ON EACH STATEMENT.

Rating Scale-

6. Always perform this task
5. Usually perform this task
4. Frequently perform task
3. Occasionally perform task
2. Seldom perform this task
1. Never perform this task-

1. I offer facts, provide relevant information and give my opinions, ideas and suggestions so the team discussion will take off.

    6_____5 _____4 _____3 _____2_____1_____

2. I encourage all members of the group to participate, demonstrate a receptivity and openness to their ideas and recognize them for their contributions.

    6_____5 _____4 _____3 _____2_____1_____

3 I ask for facts, information, opinions from team members to help the group discussion move forward so issues are solved and plans made.

    6_____5 _____4 _____3 _____2_____1_____

4. I persuade members to analyze constructively their differences of opinion and proposals and come up with the best ideas and plans for the organization.

    6_____5 _____4 _____3 _____2_____1_____

5. I set the stage for the meeting, push the group to develop objectives so we know what needs to be accomplished and how and when are we are going to meet the objectives.

    6_____5 _____4 _____3 _____2_____1_____

6. I relieve group tension and increase team cohesiveness by being positive, having a sense of humor, proposing fun approaches to group work and taking breaks at the appropriate times.

    6_____5 _____4 _____3 _____2_____1_____

7. I give direction to the group by developing steps on how the group will proceed and by having each member focus on the tasks that need to be done to meet the objectives

     6_____5 _____4 _____3 _____2_____1_____

8. I help communication among group members by showing good communication skills and by making sure that what each member says is understood by all

     6_____5 _____4 _____3 _____2_____1_____

9. I pull together related ideas or suggestions made by group members and restate and summarize the major points made by them.

     6_____5 _____4 _____3 _____2_____1_____

10. I share my knowledge about group work, the way members should interact with each other. and when it is appropriate to twitter or talk on cell phones during meetings. I also ask members how they are feeling about the way in which the group is working together.

     6_____5 _____4 _____3 _____2_____1_____

(LEADING A TEAM UNIT OR GROUP MEETING CONTINUED)

READ THE FOLLOWING 20 STATEMENTS AND RATE YOUR SELF ON EACH STATEMENT.

Rating Scale-

6. Always perform this task

5. Usually perform this task

4. Frequently perform task

3. Occasionally perform task

2. Seldom perform this task

1. Never perform this task

11. I like to work in a collaborative way pulling everyone's ideas and suggestions together to create better plans and ways of doing things.

    6_____5 _____4 _____3 _____2_____1_____

12. I am constantly observing the progress of the group and how effective it is working together.

    6_____5 _____4 _____3 _____2_____1_____

13. I can determine the impediments that are slowing the group down in achieving their goals and objectives.

    6_____5 _____4 _____3 _____2_____1_____

14. I continuously inform the group of it's progress so they know where they are in a point in time and how hard and smart they have to work to meet the predetermined objectives.

    6_____5 _____4 _____3 _____2_____1_____

15. I energize the group members by challenging them to produce a higher quality of work.

    6_____5 _____4 _____3 _____2_____1_____

16..I listen to and weigh the ideas of group members and accept their plan when I think it is well thought out and a wise one.

    6_____5 _____4 _____3 _____2_____1_____

17. I evaluate how practical and workable ideas might be, will test a theory in a real situation to see how it might work and create alternative solutions to problems when it is wise to do so.

    6_____5 _____4 _____3 _____2_____1_____

18.. I accept and support the openness of group members and reinforce individuals taking risks as long as their mistake doesn't destroy the organization.

    6_____5 _____4 _____3 _____2_____1_____

19. I continually compare our group's decisions and accomplishments with past group's standards and accomplishments so I know we are learning from the past and making progress.

6_____ 5 _____ 4 _____ 3 _____ 2 _____ 1_____

20. I promote the open and civil discussion of disagreements between group members in order to resolve issues, learn and increase team play.

6_____ 5 _____ 4 _____ 3 _____ 2_____ 1_____

Calculate Your Functioning Level on *Task Leadership* Behavior

Listed below are 10 statements that define the task functions of team leadership behavior. Please review the odd numbers on the survey you filled out and if you answered a 6, write 15 points by the statement number, if you scored a 5, write 12 points by the statement number, if you scored a 4, write 9 points by the statement number, if you scored 3, write 6 by the statement number, if you scored 2, write 3 by the statement number, if you scored 1, write 0 by the statement number. You can rate the level you are functioning on the **task function** by adding up your total scores and see where you fall below.

YOUR TASK LEADERSHIP BEHAVIOR

TASK LEADERSHIP FUNCTIONING SCORE

_____ 1. **INFORMATION AND OPINION GIVER:** OFFERS FACTS, OPINIONS, IDEAS, SUGGESTIONS AND RELEVANT INFORMATION TO HELP GROUP DISCUSSION.

_____ 3. **INFORMATION AND OPINION SEEKER:** ASKS FOR FACTS, INFORMATION, OPINIONS, IDEAS AND FEELINGS FROM OTHER MEMBERS TO HELP GROUP DISCUSSION AND TOGETHERNESS.

_____ 5. **STARTER:** PROPOSES OBJECTIVES, ACTION STEPS AND TASKS TO INITIATE ACTION WITHIN THE GROUP.

_____ 7. **DIRECTION GIVER:** DEVELOPS PLANS ON HOW TO PROCEED AND FOCUSES ATTENTION ON THE TASKS TO BE COMPLETED.

_____ 9. **SUMMARIZER:** PULLS TOGETHER RELATED IDEAS OR SUGGESTIONS AND RESTATES AND SUMMARIZES MAJOR POINTS DISCUSSED.

_____ 11. **COORDINATOR:** SHOWS RELATIONSHIPS AMONG VARIOUS IDEAS BY PULLING THEM TOGETHER AND HARMONIZES ACTIVITIES OF VARIOUS SUBGROUPS AND MEMBERS.

_____ 13. **DIAGNOSES:** FIGURES OUT THE SOURCES OF DIFFICULTIES THE GROUP HAS IN WORKING EFFECTIVELY TOGETHER AND THE IMPEDIMENTS THAT BLOCK THE TEAMS EFFORTS TO MEET THE OBJECTIVES.

_____ 15. **ENERGIZER:** BRINGS OUT ENERGY IN OTHERS AND STIMULATES A HIGHER QUALITY OF WORK FROM THE TEAM.

_____ 17. **REALITY TESTER:** EXAMINES THE PRACTICALITY AND WORKABILITY OF IDEAS, IDENTIFIES ALTERNATIVE SOLUTIONS AND APPLIES THEM TO REAL SITUATIONS TO SEE IF THEY WORK

_____19.	**EVALUATOR:** COMPARES GROUP DECISIONS AND ACCOMPLISHMENTS WITH THE TEAM'S PAST STANDARDS.

_____TOTAL SCORE - WHAT LEVEL ARE YOU FUNCTIONING? _____

LEVEL 5 (*150 TO 120)*
LEVEL 4 (120 TO 90)
LEVEL 3 (90 TO 60)
LEVEL 2 (60 TO 30)
LEVEL 1 (30 TO 0)

Calculate Your Functioning Level on *Maintenance Leadership* Behavior

Listed below are 10 statements that define the maintenance functions of team leadership behavior. Please review the even numbers on the survey you filled out and if you answered a 6, write 15 points by the statement number, if you scored a 5, write 12 points by the statement number, if you scored a 4, write 9 points by the statement number, if you scored 3, write 6 by the statement number, if you scored 2, write 3 by the statement, if you scored 1, write 0 by the statement number. You can identify the level you are functioning on the maintenance function by adding up your total score and see where you fall below.

YOUR MAINTENANCE/TEAM BUILDING LEADERSHIP BEHAVIOR

TEAM MAINTENANCE FUNCTIONING SCORE

_____2.   **ENCOURAGER OF PARTICIPATION**: WARMLY ENCOURAGES EVERYONE TO PARTICIPATE, GIVING RECOGNITION FOR CONTRIBUTIONS, DEMONSTRATING ACCEPTANCE AND OPENNESS TO IDEAS OF OTHERS.

_____4.   **HARMONIZER AND COMPROMISER**: PERSUADES MEMBERS TO ANALYZE CONSTRUCTIVELY THEIR DIFFERENCES OF OPINIONS, SEARCHES FOR COMMON ELEMENTS IN CONFLICTS AND TRIES TO RECONCILE THEM.

_____6.   **TENSION RELIEVER**: EASES TENSIONS AND INCREASES THE ENJOYMENT OF GROUP MEMBERS BY JOKING, DEMONSTRATING A SENSE OF HUMOR, SUGGESTING BREAKS AND PROPOSING FUN APPROACHES TO GROUP WORK.

_____8.   **COMMUNICATION HELPER**: SHOWS GOOD COMMUNICATION SKILLS AND MAKES SURE THAT EACH GROUP MEMBER UNDERSTANDS WHAT OTHER MEMBERS ARE SAYING.

_____10.   **EVALUATOR OF EMOTIONAL CLIMATE**: SPOT DISSONACE BETWEEN GROUP MEMBERS AND ASK MEMBERS HOW THEY FEEL ABOUT SHARING IN THE GROUP.

_____12.   **PROCESS OBSERVER**: WATCHES THE PROCESS BY WHICH THE GROUP IS WORKING AND USES THE OBSERVATIONS TO FACILITATE GROUP EFFECTIVENESS.

_____14.   **STANDARD SETTER**: EXPRESSES GROUP STANDARDS AND OBJECTIVES TO MAKE MEMBERS AWARE OF THE DIRECTION OF THE WORK AND THE PROGRESS BEING MADE TOWARD THE OBJECTIVES. SEEKS ACCEPTANCE OF GROUP NORMS AND PROCEDURES. SUCH AS NO TEXTING AND CALLS DURING A MEETING.

_____16.   **ACTIVE LISTENER**: LISTENS AND SERVES AS AN INTERESTED AUDIENCE FOR OTHER MEMBERS, IS RECEPTIVE TO OTHER IDEAS, GOES ALONG WITH THE TEAM WHEN NOT IN DISAGREEMENT

_____18.   **TRUST BUILDER**: ACCEPTS AND SUPPORTS OPENNESS OF OTHER GROUP MEMBERS, REINFORCING RISK TAKING AND ENCOURAGING INDIVIDUALITY.

_____20.   **INTERPERSONAL PROBLEM SOLVER:** MEET ONE ON ONE WITH EACH GROUP
MEMBER AND DISCUSS THE PROBLEMS THAT THEY MAY BE HAVING WITH SOMEONE
IN THE GROUP. YOU CAN DISCUSS HOW YOU WOULD APPRECIATE THE TWO OF THEM
WORKING TOGETHER TO CHANGE THE GROUP INTO A TEAM.

_____**TOTAL SCORE- WHAT LEVEL ARE YOU**
FUNCTIONING? _____
**LEVEL 5 (150 TO 120) LEVEL 4 (120 TO 90) LEVEL 3 (90 TO 60) LEVEL 2 (60 TO 30) LEVEL 1
(30 TO 0)**

Identify How You Behave in a Group /Team Meeting

Instructions: There are twenty four verbs listed below that describe some of the ways in which people feel and act in group and team meetings.

Write the **six verbs below** that best describe your behavior when you are **leading a group** or team unit meeting.

1._____   2._____   3._____   4._____   5._____   6._____

Write the **six verbs below** that best describe your behavior when you are **a member participating** in a team meeting and not leading the group session.

1._____   2._____   3._____   4._____   5._____   6._____

1) Acquiesce	2) Advise	3) Agree
4) Argue	5) Assist	6) Concede
7) Concur	8) Congenial	9) Coordinate
10) Criticize	11) Direct	12) Disapprove
13) Evade	14) Initiate	15) Judge
16) Lead	17) Object	18) Oblige
19) Passive	20) Persuade	21) Relinquish
22) Resist	23) Retreat	24) Withdraw

Review the next page and see where you fell in the four zones. Do you need to change your behavior to be a more effective team unit and team member leader?

Copyright © 2018 Michael V. Mulligan

Identify Your Team Unit and Team Member Behavior in Groups

In the boxes below, circle the six verbs you marked to describe your behavior when leading a team or group.

In which zone did you land? _____

In the boxes below, put an x through the six verbs you marked to describe your behavior when you are a member of a team or group.

In which zone did you land? _____

	Like To Control (High Dominance)	Let Others Control (Low Dominance)
Warm and Personal (High Sociability)	Advise Coordinate Direct Initiate Lead Persuade *Zone 1*	Acquiesce Agree Assist Oblige Concur Congenial *Zone 2*
Cold and Impersonal (Low Sociability)	Argue Criticize Disapprove Judge Resist Object *Zone 3*	Concede Evade Relinquish Retreat Withdraw Passive *Zone 4*

The zone in which three or more verbs are circled out of the six represent your interpersonal pattern tendencies in a group or on a team.

- Did you fall in the same zone as a team unit and team member leader?

- Should your behavior be different when playing the two leadership roles?

- What did you learn about yourself from this exercise?

Copyright © 2018 Michael V. Mulligan

111

Task # Two-

Analyze Team Dynamics by Assessing Team Members

A team unit leader should understand the group dynamics of his/her team unit so he/she can build team cohesiveness and a strong working relationship among the team members. There are two dimensions that a successful team unit must possess. These include being able to solidify relationships and achieve tasks. If the team unit does not have group cohesiveness, it will be difficult to move forward to accomplish difficult and challenging tasks. It also means you as the team leader must develop rapport and cohesiveness with your direct reports to manage them One –On- One. The better the parts fit on a car, the faster that vehicle can go without falling apart. The same concept applies to a team unit.

Team unit leaders need to understand how the parts or various personalities in his or her team fit together. This is why we put **Task Two** in **Section Three**. If you understand the personality of each member on your team, you can manage them better in One-On- One meetings and conduct constructive team meetings.

You can use one or all three of the following assessment tools to understand each direct report and the personality differences of the people on your team. You should tell your direct reports that you always assess your staff so you can learn the group dynamics of the team and help them work together. A career coach from Mulligan & Associates can provide the personality surveys to your direct reports and interpret the results to you and them. They can take one or all the following surveys.

- **The Team Unit Group Dynamics Survey-**
  You filled this survey out on last few pages but you should have your direct reports fill it out as well.
- **The Mulligan Leadership Personality Profile**
  Mulligan & Associates Inc. can give you copies of this survey and you can give them to your staff to fill out and self score.
- **The Myers Briggs Type Indicator®**
  Mulligan & Associates Inc. can give you copies of the MBTI to give to your direct reports to fill out and M&A can score them.

The Team Unit Group Dynamics Survey

As a way of reviewing the interpersonal patterns or group dynamics of your team unit, you should have direct reports complete the interpersonal pattern exercise below.

Instructions: There are twenty verbs listed below that describe some of the ways in which people feel and act in groups. Please think of your behavior in regards to how you normally act in your group. Check the five verbs below that best describe your behavior in your team unit.

__ Acquiesce	__ Coordinate	__ Initiate	__ Retreat
__ Advise	__ Concur	__ Judge	__ Withdrawl
__ Agree	__ Criticize	__ Lead	
__ Analyze	__ Direct	__ Oblige	
__ Assist	__ Disapprove	__ Relinquish	
__ Concede	__ Evade	__ Resist	

In every group, you will have those that want to dominate and those that allow themselves to be dominated. You will have people who are innovative and those that like to do it the same way every time. You will have people who are more sociable and talkative and those who are more reserved and quiet. You will have people who are more cautious and those who are impulsive, people who are direct in analyzing problems and those who are polite and sensitive to others. You will have those who like structure and those who like change. In which zones did each person on the team fall? See next page. Were there any surprises?

The Team Unit Group Dynamics Survey Results

In the box below, circle the five verbs you used to describe yourself in group activity.

	Like To Control (High Dominance)	Let Others Control (Low Dominance)
Warm and Personal (High Sociability)	Advise Coordinate Direct Initiate Lead *Zone 1*	Acquiesce Agree Assist Oblige Concur *Zone 2*
Cold and Impersonal (Low Sociability)	Argue Criticize Disapprove Judge Resist *Zone 3*	Concede Evade Relinquish Retreat Withdraw *Zone 4*

The set in which three or more verbs are circled out of the five represent your interpersonal pattern tendencies in groups.

- In which zone did you as the team leader fall?
- In which zone did each of your direct reports fall?
- What have you learned about the personality differences of your team?
- What adjustments will each direct report have to make to build a more cohesive sharing team?

The challenge of any team is to work together as a team. John Wooden, one of the greatest college basketball coaches ever, led the UCLA Bruins to ten national championships. The key to the Bruins success was Coach Woodens unyielding dedication to his concept of teamwork. There was a picture of John Wooden in *Sports Illustrated* many years ago and under the picture, the caption read, "The guy who puts the ball through the hoop has ten hands. The strong winds of resistance facing many teams are the players themselves. **One factor** is the personality and the diversity make-up of the team. The **second factor** is how each player reacts to each other. A **third** and extremely important factor is attitude. If you can work and perform as a team, your chances for being successful in life and a career will improve.

The Mulligan Leadership Personality Profile

Where does everyone on the team fall on the Mulligan Leadership Assessment Profile? .
You can place each person's initials where they landed in the box levels below and on the
following pages. The higher the score and level, the more the individuals are like the traits
described. Those individuals who fall at level 5 and 4 on competitiveness, determination
and self directed scales are those who should be considered for the top leadership positions
in the company. They like setting the performance bar high and pushing others to be the
best in their field. They have a high want and will to win. However they could need help in
other areas.

Three Line Position Traits Needed to Push Performance Bar Higher

Competitive/High Want to Achieve   **Team Mean Score_____**

Measuring Traits	Definitely Like You	Usually Like You	Somewhat Like You	A Little Like You	Not Like You
-Competitive -Aggressive -Entrepreneurial -High Standards -Prospect For The Business	*Level 5*	**Level 4**	**Level 3**	**Level 2**	**Level 1**

Determined/High Will to Achieve   **Team Mean Score _____**

Measuring Traits	Definitely Like You	Usually Like You	Somewhat Like You	A Little Like You	Not Like You
-Persistence -Sense of Urgency -Dependable -Close the Sale -Hard driving -Intense -Focused	*Level 5*	**Level 4**	**Level 3**	**Level 2**	**Level 1**

Willing to Go It Alone/Self Directed   **Team Mean Score** _____

Measuring Traits	Definitely Like You	Usually Like You	Somewhat Like You	A Little Like You	Not Like You
-Self directed -Independent -Strong minded -Work Alone -Self Manager -Self Starter	*Level 5*	**Level 4**	**Level 3**	**Level 2**	**Level 1**

Five Support or Staff Position Traits

Detail Oriented   **Team Mean Score** _____

Measuring Traits	Definitely Like You	Usually Like You	Somewhat Like You	A Little Like You	Not Like You
-Technical -Researcher -Precise/Analytic -No Mistakes -Organized -Factual	*Level 5*	**Level 4**	**Level 3**	**Level 2**	**Level 1**

Patient/In Self Control   **Team Mean Score** _____

Measuring Traits	Definitely Like You	Usually Like You	Somewhat Like You	A Little Like You	Not Like You
-Patient -Less intense -Relaxed -Doesn't get rattled -Calm -Steady	*Level 5*	**Level 4**	**Level 3**	**Level 2**	**Level 1**

Helper/ Performance Facilitator   Team Mean Score _____

Measuring Traits	Definitely Like You	Usually Like You	Somewhat Like You	A Little Like You	Not Like You
-Caring -Trustworthy -Attending Skills -Empathic -Listening Skills Help Person Understand Situation and Execute a Plan -High E.Q.	*Level 5*	**Level 4**	**Level 3**	**Level 2**	**Level 1**

Innovative/Creative   Team Mean Score _____

Measuring Traits	Definitely Like You	Usually Like You	Somewhat Like You	A Little Like You	Not Like You
-Visionary -Strategic -Curious -Critical Thinker -Likes Improving Processes - Brainstorming	*Level 5*	**Level 4**	**Level 3**	**Level 2**	**Level 1**

Team Builder/Player   Team Mean Score _____

Measuring Traits	Definitely Like You	Usually Like You	Somewhat Like You	A Little Like You	Not Like You
-Collaborative -Like to Share -Team Oriented - Team Player -Open Minded -Puts Others in Spot Light	*Level 5*	**Level 4**	**Level 3**	**Level 2**	**Level 1**

Who were the individuals with level 5 and 4 scores on:

- **competitiveness**

- **determination**

- **self directness**

- **helper**

Who were the individuals with 5 and 4 scores on:

- **detail**

- **patience**

- **innovative**

- **team orientation**

Myers- Briggs Type Indicator Inventory®

Mulligan & Associates Inc. can administer the MBTI® to you and your direct reports.

Distribution of Scores

Please place the initials of your direct reports under the corresponding categories:

E Extraversion	I Introversion
S Sensing	N Intuition
T Thinking	F Feeling
J Judging	P Perceiving

ISTJ	ISFJ	INFJ	INTJ
ISTP	ISFP	INFP	INTP
ESTP	ESFP	ENFP	ENTP
ESTJ	ESFJ	ENFJ	ENTJ

Understanding What Each Personality Trait Means

Where you get your energy – Extraverts vs. Introverts

Extraverts observe and make decisions in the *outer* world of other people. They are energized by people and action. They become drained if they spend too much time alone. They tend to talk rather than listen.

Introverts tend to keep their observations and decisions *inside*. They are energized by thoughts and ideas. They become drained if they spend too much time with other people. They tend to listen rather than talk.

How you gather information – Sensors vs. Intuitors

Sensors gather information in a hands-on, sequential way. They are interested in the tangible, here-and-now aspects of a situation, and do not feel the need to interpret facts. They prefer details and specifics.

Intuitors gather information in a more figurative, random way. They are less concerned with the thing itself than what the thing means. They look for possibilities and relationships between and among things. They tend to look at the "big picture."

How you make decisions – *Thinking vs. Feeling*

Thinkers make decisions logically and objectively. They base their decisions on data and analyses and tend not to get personally involved in a decision.

Feelers make decisions subjectively. How the decisions will impact other people is very important. The decision-making process is driven by interpersonal involvement.

How you orient your life – *Judgers vs. Perceivers*

Judgers prefer a planned and orderly lifestyle. They structure their environment and prefer to plan activities in advance. There's usually a "right way" and a "wrong way" to do anything.

Perceivers prefer to be flexible and spontaneous. They create and environment that is adaptive and responsive. They tend to keep collecting information rather than draw conclusions. They take a "wait and see" attitude on most things.

Team Distribution and Definitions

Extraverts

- Are energized by being with other people
- Like being the center of attention
- Act, then think
- Tend to think out loud

- Are easier to "read" and know; share personal information freely

- Talk more than listen
- Communicate with enthusiasm
- Respond quickly; enjoy a fast pace

- Prefer breadth to depth

Number of team members with this trait

_____

Notes:

Introverts

- Are energized by spending time alone
- Avoid being the center of attention
- Think, then act
- Think things through inside their heads

- Are more passive; prefer to share personal information with a select few

- Listen more than talk
- Keep their enthusiasm to themselves
- Respond after taking the time to think things through

- Prefer depth to breadth

Number of team members with this trait

Sensors

- Trust is certain and concrete
- Like new ideas only if they have practical applications
- Value realism and common sense
- Like to use and hone established skills

- Tend to be specific and literal; give detailed description
- Present information in a step-by-step manner
- Are oriented to the present

Number of team members with this trait

_____

Intuitive

- Trust inspiration and inference
- Like new ideas and concepts for their own sake
- Value imagination and innovation
- Like to learn new skills; get bored easily after mastering skills

- Tend to be general and figurative; use metaphors and analogies
- Present information through leaps, in a roundabout manner
- Are oriented toward the future

Number of team members with this trait

_____

121

Thinkers

- Step back; apply impersonal analysis to problems
- Value logic, justice, and fairness; one standard for all
- Naturally see flaws and tend to be critical
- May be seen as heartless, insensitive, and uncaring
- Consider it more important to be truthful than tactful
- Believe feelings are valid only if they are logical
- Are motivated by a desire for achievement and accomplishment

Feelers

- Step forward; consider effect of actions on others
- Value empathy and harmony; see the exception to the rule
- Naturally like to please others; show appreciation easily
- May be seen as overemotional, illogical, and weak
- Consider it important to be tactful as well as truthful
- Believe any feeling is valid, whether it makes sense or not
- Are motivated by a desire to be appreciated

Number of team members with this trait
_____

Number of team members with this trait
_____

Judgers

- Are happiest after decisions have been made
- Have a "work ethic": work first, play later (if there's time)
- Set goals and work toward achieving them on time
- Prefer knowing what they are getting into
- Are product oriented (emphasis is on completing the task)
- Derive satisfaction from finishing projects
- See time as a finite resource and take deadlines seriously

Perceivers

- Are happiest leaving their options open
- Have a "play ethic": enjoy now, finish the job later (if there's time)
- Change goals as new information becomes available
- Like adapting to new situations
- Are process oriented (emphasis is on how the task is completed)
- Derive satisfaction from starting projects
- See time as a renewable resource and see deadlines as elastic

Number of team members with this trait
_____

Number of team members with this trait
_____

Helpful Suggestions for Team Members That Fall Under These Categories

Extraverts

- Give people time to think.
- Don't fill all silences with words.
- Listen to ideas before you react.
- Put agendas and reports into writing before the meeting.
- Say, "Let me recap what you've just said to make sure I've heard it correctly."
- Make sure everyone has the chance to express his or her opinion.
- Remember: Silence doesn't always mean consent.

Introverts

- Let Extraverts speak their minds without always holding them to what they say.
- Sharing more than just your final conclusion.
- Don't assume your thoughts are too trivial to say out loud.
- Develop nonverbal signals – nodding you head, smiling, whatever – to indicate your assent or dissent.
- Try saying, "I would normally keep this to myself, however, let me share that the proposal in is present seems a little weak."

Sensors

- Don't dismiss "farfetched" ideas too early.
- Allow others to ramble on for awhile.
- Keep in mind that the very idea of goal setting involves pondering the future. You might prefer to get busy actually doing something, but that time will come.
- Try saying, "I think this may be pie in the sky, but let's talk it through."

Intuitives

- Remember the details.
- Keep in touch with reality.
- When giving feedback, try to be specific.
- When asking for feedback, avoid generalities like "What do you think?" in favor of specific requests: "I'd like some feedback on items one and four."

Thinkers

- Pay attention to points of view that seem on the schmaltzy side.
- Keep in mind that how you work together as a group is as important as what you accomplish.
- Try saying, "How will this goal affect the people who must carry it out?"

- Not everyone appreciates a healthy discussion of aggressively pursuing a point for the sake of argument. That will cause some of your team members to drop out of the process.
- Reaching a goal isn't worth pursuing if you alienate everyone getting there.

Feelers
- It's okay to disagree.
- While harmony is important, every issue can't always be resolved with everyone feeling good.
- Not every work spoken about a suggestion you make is directed personally at you.
- Try saying, "This goal makes sense on the bottom line, and therefore personal differences should be set aside."
- Goals can be reached even if everyone isn't in total agreement.

Judgers
- Allow time for a variety of opinions to be discussed; don't settle on the first good idea you hear.
- Remember that not all goals can be reached immediately, nor should they be.
- Don't assume that those who disagree with your goals aren't committed to them.
- Try saying, "That's okay for now, but let's wait before we make a final decision."

Perceivers
- Try to settle on something and live with it awhile before redesigning it.
- State what you think about a goal as directly as possible.
- Making a firm decision and sticking to it isn't the end of the world.
- Remind yourself that some goals can be reached one day at a time. The small, short-term accomplishments are as important as the bigger ones.
- Try saying, "It's a closed issue. Let's move on to something else."

Task # Three-

Learn and Execute the TEAM Program
(Team Engagement Achievement Motivation)

One of the best ways to build rapport with your direct reports and bring them board is to challenge them. You should tell them you are interested in their career development and advancement and you want them to transform themselves and the organization into the *Best in their Field*. You want them to develop their potential to the fullest and be recognized as star performers in the company and in their profession.

Abraham Maslow and Carl Rogers, psychologists, stated that the majority of people use about 10% or 15% of their potential[3]. There a number of reasons for this fact.

- Seven out of every 10 statements made each day by people are usually critical or negative about someone or a situation. This negative communication makes people play it safe. If you don't do anything more than you are asked to do, you reduce the chances of being criticized.
- Many of us don't take advantage of the educational programs that are offered to us in school or at work.
- We don't know our strengths and potential. We need to identify our strengths and use them to the fullest so we can become what we want to be.
- We should not hide our weaknesses as we all have them. We need to identify weaknesses and transform them into strengths.

"If you treat a person as he/she is, he/she will remain as they are. If you treat a person as they ought to be and should be, they will become what they ought to be and should be." *Goethe*

Getting Started
You can use the *Team Engagement Achievement Motivation Program* to build team unity, and motivate your direct reports to become the *Best in Their Field*. Someone from Mulligan & Associates Inc. or your organization can conduct the first couple of team session for you. We suggest you sit down together as a team at the beginning of the year and cover eight activities. Once you complete the activities, establish individual and team objectives and tasks you would like to achieve for the year.

Your team can meet twice a month to discuss how you and your team as a whole are meeting your growth objectives and tasks. We can review the seven activities with you ahead of time so you the team unit leader feel comfortable with the topics that will be discussed. By doing this, we can add discussion activities and subtract the ones you do not want to introduce to your team unit. The seven activities are listed below.

The **Seven Activities** include:

Activity One - *Learning to Share and Communicate with One Another*-The Key to building rapport, working relationships and being successful.

Activity Two - *Sharing Successes and Meaningful Experiences*-As a person studies his own history of success, he can define success for the present and future.

Activity Three - *Identifying Your Strengths Based on Past Success*- Everyone has unrecognized strengths that will be reflected in his/her pattern of success. As the strengths are identified, they can be used effectively as a helper to others and the unit.

Activity Four -*Building a Confidence Base.* The primary objective of the TEAM program is to enable reports to take positive action in selecting and accomplishing goals. We want to enhance one's self concept. The increased sense of self worth provides the power base for one to launch into new and desirable activities.

Activity Five - *Team Planning*- Review the vision, mission and objectives of the organization and then develop your vision, mission and objectives that, if met, would transform your team unit into the best in its functional area.

Activity Six – *Conduct Team Monthly Meetings* to monitor the teams progress, meeting objectives and wave the Team Flag

Activity One

Learning To Share - The Key to an Effective Working Relationship

A sharing relationship is the cornerstone to building an effective working relationship. The five core conditions are:

1) **TRUST**: I can tell this person something and he/she will use the information to help me in some way. They will keep what I say to themselves. Confidentiality is a necessary condition for eliciting discussion and effective communication.

2) **CARING**: I feel this person cares for me. He/she make me feel important as they are always listening carefully to what I have to say. He or she is genuinely interested in my welfare and growth.

3) **EMPATHIC**: This person can respond to my feelings helping me work through my emotional states. He or she does not put me on the defensive or treat me in a robotic way.

4) **RESPECT**: This person believes in me and my capabilities. He or she encourages me to use my potential and talent. These individuals know I can solve my own problems, make plans and execute them.

5) **DEVELOPING A COMMON GROUND**: We have the same interests, goals, values and like doing some of the same things. We all face the same challenges and we have developed a mission that unites us. We want to maximize our high school and college education and prepare ourselves for a career and life.

There are several reasons why people do not share information with each other. Some of these include:

- I am a very private person
- I don't trust what people will do with the information.
- I don't have much to say.
- I don't feel comfortable sharing with certain people.

DISCUSSION

- Are you good at sharing information with your boss, direct reports, colleagues, friends, customers and spouse?
- Do you think most of us are good at sharing information about ourselves?
- If not, how can we communicate better?
- What are your thoughts about sharing?

127

SHARING INFORMATION ABOUT SELF TO YOUR TEAM MATES

As a way of your team mates getting to know you, we would like each of you to share some personal information on the following six topics.

Topic One -   Discuss your Name

Topic Two -   A snapshot of your life

Topic Three -   The Most Influential People In Your Life

Topic Four -   One of the Funniest Experiences in Your Life

Topic Five -   Things That Make You Happy

Topic Six -   Your Proudest Moment

Your team should take one topic at a time and put a time limit on how long each person will discuss the topic. This process gives everyone equal time to talk. Please have a different person start each time. After the first person shares, go to the next person until everyone on the team has had the opportunity to speak. A timer should be appointed to keep everyone within the designated timelines. No one dominates the conversation.

TOPIC ONE: Discuss Your Name (90 seconds per person)

One of the most important ways to build relationships with someone is to identify them by their appropriate name and pronounce it correctly. Many times we are so busy that we don't take the time to introduce or address people properly. If we can't remember their name, we might not introduce them at all. By taking the time to find out how people like to be addressed, you will find your personal power increasing with others. Each team member should share the following:

- Their Full Name
- The story behind how they got their name.
- Your nick name and how you got this name.
- How you like to be introduced.
- What you want to be called by team mates
- How you feel when someone calls you be the wrong name or doesn't introduce you correctly?

Sharing Information about Self to Your Teammates Continued

TOPIC TWO: Give Your Team Mates a Snapshot of Your Life
(two minutes)

Provide a brief background of your life and remember the most interesting thing about life is people. You are a unique person with relevant things to say about yourself. Let your team mates learn the personal side of you. Some of the areas to cover would include:

- Place of birth.
- Name of parents and occupations.
- Siblings.
- Places you have lived.
- What you liked about your siblings and parents..
- Ultimate career aspirations at this time.
- Things you like to do when not working.
- How you think individuals should help others.

TOPIC THREE: Discuss the Most Influential People in Your Life
(90 seconds per person)

Discuss two or three people who have made an impact on your life and how.

TOPIC FOUR: Some of Your Funniest Experiences in Life
(90 seconds per person)

All of us have experienced a time in our lives in which something happened to us that was really funny. What was your most memorable experience?

TOPIC FIVE: The Things That Make You Happy
(90 seconds per person)

This is a question that all of us keep asking ourselves. Please share with your team mates what you think makes you happy.

TOPIC SIX: Your Proudest Moment
(90 seconds per person)

Identify and discuss the proudest moment in your life and tell why.

Activity Two

Sharing Successes and Meaningful Experiences

At this time, we will ask each person on the team to share some of their successes and growth experiences. Remember, there are many types of successes. One person met his performance objectives at work while another person saved enough money to pay for his children's college education. Both individuals met their objectives and felt good about their achievements. A meaningful experience could be failing at something or have a bad experience and learn from it.

We build on our successes. One success leads to another but we should remember a lot of famous people didn't succeed at everything. They also had some failures. We are continually learning as we go through life.

Each person on the team will have the opportunity to share their successes and meaningful experiences with their team mates. We have four rounds where each person on the team can share. Each person will have two minutes in each round to share.

Round One - Each team member will discuss their successes and the growth experiences they have had in school- junior high, senior high, college.

Round Two - Each team member will discuss how they have helped members of their family, friends, people in their neighborhood, community.

Round Three - Each team member will share with their team mates their major successes at work.

Round Four - Each team member will discuss where they have grown the most over the years and where they want to grow in the future.

Round Five- Each person will share where they did not meet their expectations and learned from it.

YOUR SUCCESSES AND GROWTH EXPERIENCES

Round One- School – Junior High, Senior High and College
(two minutes per person)
>   1)
>
>   2)
>
>   3)

Round Two- Helping Others (two minutes per person)
>   1)
>
>   2)
>
>   3)

Round Three- Biggest Achievements at Work (two minutes per person)
>   1)
>
>   2)
>
>   3)

Round Four- Where I Have Grown the Most and Where I Want to Grow in the Future (two minutes per person)
>   1)
>
>   2)
>
>   3)

Round Five- Where Did You Fail and What Did You Learn From It?
>   1)
>
>   2)
>
>   3)

Activity Three

Identifying Your Team Mates Strengths

You have heard each of your teammates share information about themselves. As you listened to each person, you started to see positive things about them. At this time, we would like you to identify the strengths of each of your team mates as you see them. Gallup through its research found when an organizations leadership focuses on the strengths of its employees, the odds of their success soars.

DIRECTIONS

1) We ask each team member to pass this manual to the person on his or her right. This person will act as a recorder.

2) Focus on one team mate at a time for two minutes to identify their strengths.

3) Each team member will look the person in the spot light in the eye address him or her by their name and tell them about a strength they possess. Each person making the statement should be completely honest and genuine.

4) The strengths will be recorded on the following page by the recorder. The team should go around two or three times giving everyone the opportunity to share more than one strength. The recorder will write down all the strengths of the person in the spotlight.

5) After the first person received feedback from the team, put another person in the spotlight until everyone has had a turn. Each teammate should try to be as precise as possible when stating the strengths of their teammates.

6) When your team mates make comments to you, just listen and not say anything. You should take in how people view your strengths.

Your Name

_____

Your Strengths as Perceived by Your Teammates- Record Below

Your Strengths as Perceived by You

Activity Four

Discuss Your Confidence Base to Move Forward

Questions:

- How do you react to all the positive statements made about you?

- Do you think that if people complimented others more often, it would improve their confidence base and they would take more chances at work? How often should a person be complimented?

- On a scale of 1 to 10, 1 being low and 10 being high, at what level is your confidence base today?

- If people gave out "Mulligans" - second chances - do you think you would take more risks?

<u>Activity Five</u>

Team Planning
Develop Team Objectives that, if met, Will
Transform Your Team Unit into Best in Its Functional Area

Provide each direct report with the vision and mission statements and goals of the organization and let the team discuss the vision and mission statements and rank the goals in terms of importance to the team unit. You can go back to the page 11 of this manual and review the suggested corporate goals and objectives. You can also have direct reports rank the 40 major challenges facing the organization on next page. See if your team unit can reach consensus on the top eight goals that your team unit should meet.

<u>Goal One-</u>

<u>GoalTwo-</u>

<u>Goal Three-</u>

<u>Goal Four-</u>

<u>Goal Five-</u>

<u>Goal Six</u>

<u>Goal Seven</u>

<u>Goal Eight</u>

Listed below is an evaluation survey direct reports can fill out. You and they can discuss their evaluation. You can learn how they view the organization.

40 Major Challenges Facing Our Organization	Please rate the following challenges in terms of how effective our organization is managing them. Scale 0 – 10 0 – Not effective 10 – Extremely effective
1. Creating change agendas that are needed, communicating the agendas and gaining commitment to implement them.	
2. Developing a Leadership Empowerment and Expert Program to determine when to empower employees.	
3. Attracting, selecting and retaining employees who will help us become number one.	
4. Establishing a pay for performance incentive plan.	
5. Increasing profit and shareholder value.	
6. Developing a company vision, mission, objectives and a plan and executing the plan so we are successful.	
7. Maintaining excellent relations with present customers while increasing our customer base.	
8. Determining what businesses we want to be in.	
9. Identifying our market niche and increasing share.	
10. Developing a one-on-one management program to increase individual productivity, performance and leadership so employees and the company become the best in the field.	
11. Pursuing a cause or purpose that will unify, excite and reward everyone in the organization.	
12. Increasing quality of products/service while managing costs.	
13. Training employees how to function as skilled performance facilitators to bring out the best in themselves and others.	

14. Keeping up with the latest technology to remain competitive.	
15. Satisfying and meeting the needs of the workforce so they can better focus on achieving tasks and objectives.	
16. Building a unified workforce	
17. Containing health care costs and decreasing absenteeism at work. 112	
18. Building a "Competitive Intelligence and Learning Center" to grow individuals and beat the competition.	
19. Deciding whether to manufacture or outsource products.	
20. Establishing a participation management style to include all employees in the business planning process.	
21. Constantly striving to beat local and global competition to be number one in the marketplace.	
22. Defining and living company values.	
23. Using the expertise of retired employees.	
24. Evaluating how we communicate to each other in the organization and developing a plan to improve communication	
25. Reducing costs by hiring a combination of full time, part time and temporary employees.	
26. Establishing a career development program for all employees.	
27. Identifying performance facilitating behaviors and working with employees to turn them into everyday habits.	
28. Developing a merger and acquisition strategy to grow.	
29. Managing occupational safety and health.	
30. Establishing a program that reduces anger and lawsuits in the workplace.	
31. Developing a competency base program and creating a talent pool to be used through the organization.	
32. Managing downsizing and restructuring without reducing the enthusiasm and commitment of the workforce.	
33. Supplying the resources needed to compete and grow the company while maintaining a meaningful work environment.	

34. Developing a team leadership model so all employees know when and how to step up as leaders.	
35. Defining what is politically and ethically correct in the organization.	
36 The Board of Directors and Senior Management Team working together to lead the company	
37. Establishing a win-win situation between the union and management.	
38.Identifying future team unit leaders and building a Leadership Farm System to train them	
39. Helping employees balance work and personal life.	
40. Marketing and selling our company to the stock analysts or public.	
TOTAL POINTS	=
AVERAGE SCORE (DIVIDE BY 40 TO OBTAIN SCORE)	=

<u>Activity Six</u>

Work with Direct Reports to Identify the Objectives Under Eight Team Unit Goals They Must Meet to be Successful

List your goals and then list two objectives you must meet to reach the goal. . Ask each of direct reports to share with the team why they listed the objectives that they did.

Goal One-

    Objective One-

    Objective Two-

Goal Two-

    Objective One-

    Objective Two-

Goal Three-

    Objective One-

    Objective Two-

Goal Four-

    Objective One-

    Objective Two-

Goal Five-

    Objective One-

    Objective Two-

Goal Six-

    Objective One-

    Objective Two-

Goal Seven-

    Objective One-

    Objective Two-

Goal Eight-

    Objective One-

    Objective Two-

Activity Seven

Learn How to Wave Your Team's flag and Promote Yourself and Direct Reports

There are many companies, departments and individuals that do outstanding work today and never receive any recognition for it. You wait for others to notice your achievements, deliver the rewards you deserve, advance your career and give your company a five star rating on Wall Street.

The problem is that if you do not "wave your flag" to let people know how good you and your organization have been, you might not ever be recognized as the best in your field. You owe it to your direct reports and yourself to wave your flag. The best way to get your people behind you is to help them keep their job and be promoted.

The challenge is to develop and achieve *Best in Our Field* objectives and market your accomplishments so people perceive you as the best in your field. If you and your teammates are viewed as part of the team that built a highly successful organization, it will enhance and advance your career. Therefore, it is important to develop an action plan that will promote a positive image of you across the organization and industry.

We suggest seven ways to wave your flag. Your team should discuss all of them, select those that you like and add others that you think would be effective for your situation. The seven marketing ideas include:

1) Establish a Championship Evaluation Committee to rank you #1.
2) Develop The *Professional Promotion Program.*
3) Have employees write articles for the print media, make presentations at professional meetings and be on television for making positive contributions to the profession.
4) Initiate the *Expert Program* to promote the use of talent in the organization.
5) Establish the Community and World Help Program.
6) Use the *Partnership Expectation PAC Program* to promote yourself, department and organization.
7) Establish the *Monthly Accomplishment Program* waving your flag in the right places. Waving our flag to promote everyone on the Team

IDEA ONE

Establish a Championship Evaluation Committee to rank you #1.

The *Triangle Team Leadership Model* recommends after your organization establishes the criteria it needs to achieve to be ranked a *Best in Our Field* organization, that you select an evaluation committee to objectively rate your results and crown you #1.

You should put people on this committee that represent a cross section of partners who have an interest in the organization and would enjoy participating in the process. They should be individuals who would evaluate you all year, judge you fairly and give you the recognition you earned.

If you are selecting a committee to evaluate your entire organization, some of the people should come from:

Wall Street	Family Members
The Media	Retired Employees
Shareholders	Community
Customers	Consulting Firms
Employees	The Board of Directors
Suppliers	The International Community

If you are selecting a committee to evaluate your department, some of the people could be:

Customers	Community
Co-workers	Family Members
Suppliers	The Board of Directors
Retired Employees	your Professional Association
Senior Management	

IDEA TWO

The Professional Promotion Program

The Professional Promotion Program is designed to have teammates think of ways to promote themselves, their department and company. Teammates should encourage each other to do research, conduct special programs and become an expert on the latest issues in their field. Articles can be written in the print media, presentations can be made at professional meetings and inside the company and specific achievements by the departments and individuals can be discussed on television. This should be carefully orchestrated through the company's public relations department. Carefully print a monthly summary of your teams individual achievements like on the following page, then, take everyone's summary and put them together in a special promotion book

List some promotional ideas below.

MONTH	PLANNED & SUCCESSFUL PROMOTIONAL ACTIVITES IDENTIFY YOUR MONTHLY PROMOTIONAL PLANS AND DISCUSS SUCCESSES WITH YOUR REPORTS.
JANUARY	
FEBRUARY	
MARCH	
APRIL	
MAY	
JUNE	
JULY	
AUGUST	
SEPTEMBER	
OCTOBER	
NOVEMBER	
DECEMBER	

IDEA THREE

INITIATE THE *EXPERT PROGRAM* TO PROMOTE TALENT IN THE COMPANY & DEPARTMENT

Each manager/team unit leader should cover the five stages of the Task Expert Model when reviewing the work tasks with each employee.

    Stage #1 Identify Tasks to be Completed.
    Stage #2 Empower Direct Report to Complete Tasks He or She Can Do
    Stage #3 Help Direct Report Become Able to Complete Other Tasks.
    Stage #4 Empowers Direct Report so He/She Can Do all the Tasks Alone.
    Stage# 5 Direct Report can Unconsciously do Tasks-Becomes An Expert.

The goal is to help each partner be prepared and committed to completing each task and becoming an expert in that task area. Partners should be recognized for their expertise in a special book called "The Experts." Teammates can be listed under special expertise areas. This book can be circulated in the organization and employees with special expertise can be called upon by other Employees for help or assistance.

List your expertise on the next page and put all your teammate's lists together. If your direct reports have a short list in the beginning, you should work with them to expand their expert areas. The list should grow as the year progresses.

What are some sample expert areas you have as a team unit leader?

_____

_____

_____

_____

_____

YOUR EXPERT AREAS DESCRIBE AREA(S OF EXPERTISE

IDEA FOUR

ESTABLISHING THE "COMMUNITY AND WORLD HELP PROGRAMS"

There is much to do in helping less fortunate people in our community and world. Corporations give millions of dollars each year to charities and employees volunteer their time to many community groups. The big question is, "If 100 people in the community were asked what your organization did for the community, what would they say?" If you are doing good deeds for the community and world, what kind of publicity are you receiving for it? General Electric ran a commercial on television showing how their retired employees are part of a mentoring program to help the youth of America. This commercial enhanced the image of the company.

How is your department or company channeling its resources to help others and your organization's image?

Make a list of programs that you and your teammates could sponsor or take part in each month. Track and publicize your participation.

MONTHS	HELP PROGRAMS WE WILL CONDUCT IN THE COMMUNITY AND WORLD	CHECK BOX WHEN COMPLETED
JANUARY		☐
FEBRUARY		☐
MARCH		☐
APRIL		☐
MAY		☐
JUNE		☐
JULY		☐
AUGUST		☐
SEPTEMBER		☐
OCTOBER		☐
NOVEMBER		☐
DECEMBER		☐

IDEA FIVE

PROMOTING YOURSELF AND DEPARTMENT THROUGH THE PARTNERSHIP EXPECTATION P.A.C. PROGRAM

After you have met face-to-face with your partners inside and outside of your department to identify the expectations you have of each other, write a positive note to a minimum of three partners each month, praising where they have been most helpful. Write to all partners by the end of the year. You should write more than once during the year to those who have continuously exceeded your expectations. Your letters might come at a time when they need a pat on the back. The success of this particular activity depends on being genuine and honest in your comments when praising your partners.

MONTHS	NAME OF PARTNER RECEIVING NOTES - REASON FOR LETTER OF PRAISE
JANUARY	
FEBRUARY	
MARCH	
APRIL	
MAY	
JUNE	
JULY	
AUGUST	
SEPTEMBER	
OCTOBER	
NOVEMBER	
DECEMBER	

IDEA SIX

ESTABLISH THE *MONTHLY ACCOMPLISHMENT PROGRAM*

In order to wave your flag, you need to know what you, your department and organization have accomplished. Make a list of accomplishments for yourself, department and organization each month. This information should be summarized and circulated to the proper people. If possible, try to quantify your accomplishments. You and your teammates can develop a *Team Resume* that can be circulated within the organization at the appropriate time. The layout of the team resume is outlined below. It should be one page.

Name of Company

Address:

Qualifications Summary

A best in field sales force that exceeded its sales objectives by 20% in 2017 while increasing its customer base by 20% and market share by 18%.

Name of Department

Reports to _____   The team is accountable for:

_____

_____

Accomplishments by Team (Quantify all the accomplishments if possible):

MONTHS	MY "MOST IMPORTANT" MONTHLY ACCOMPLISHMENT- ONE PER MONTH

JANUARY	
FEBRUARY	
MARCH	
APRIL	
MAY	
JUNE	
JULY	
AUGUST	
SEPTEMBER	
OCTOBER	
NOVEMBER	
DECEMBER	

MONTHS	MY DEPARTMENT AND COMPANY'S "MOST IMPORTANT" MONTHLY ACCOMPLISHMENT Discuss With Your Teammates And Select One For Each Month
JANUARY	
FEBRUARY	
MARCH	
APRIL	
MAY	
JUNE	
JULY	
AUGUST	
SEPTEMBER	
OCTOBER	
NOVEMBER	
DECEMBER	

(IDEA SEVEN)

Waving Our Flag

You have just completed six exercises that can be meaningful as well as gain your team unit recognition. This last exercise focuses on three action plans that will insure that individuals and the team will be truly recognized for their performance and deeds. These include:

Action Plan One – The Partnership Praise Program

Action Plan Two – The Team Newsletter

Action Plan Three – Quarterly P.E.P. Rallies

The Partnership Praise Program

Action Plan 1

After teammates have discussed their accomplishments each month during The Team Meetings, teammates should take two or three minutes to praise the individual for his or her efforts, achievements and performance facilitating behavior.

Exchange books and have a reporter write the words of praise in the following circle. Genuine positive comments should be the only ones made. Repeat the process until all individuals have been in the spotlight. You should do this exercise each month if time allows. You should also do this alone with your manager.

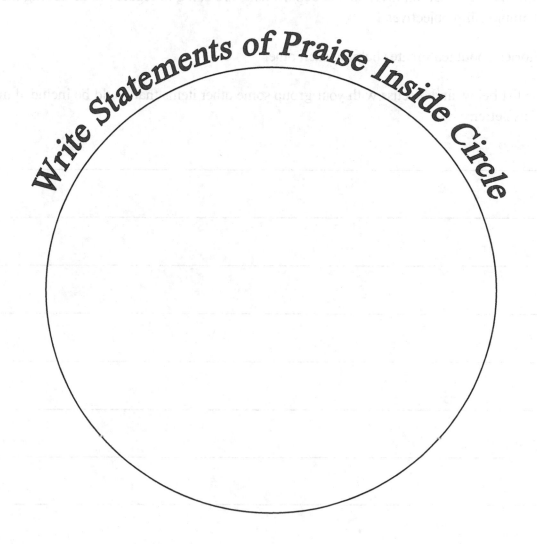

Action Plan 2

A company or department Newsletter can be written and circulated every quarter. The contents should include:

Special accomplishments by the company

Special accomplishments by the departments

Special accomplishments by individuals

Issues or challenges that need to be addressed

How the organization, division and departments are doing in regards to achieving their Championship objectives

Stories about teammates helping each other

Please list below and discuss with your group some other items that could be included in the Newsletter.

- _____

- _____

- _____

- _____

- _____

- _____

- _____

- _____

Action Plan Three

P.E.P Rallies can be for team units or the entire company. The Goals of the quarterly P.E.P. Rallies are:

- To bring everyone together to celebrate the quarterly accomplishments toward becoming a Championship Organization.
- To recognize departments and individuals for their accomplishments and leadership by example.
- To have special speeches to make people laugh and be motivated toward the Mission of Becoming the BEST IN Our Field
- To conduct team building activities that will put energy in the tanks of all employees.
- The Best in Our Field evaluation committee can appoint a P.E.P. rally committee to organize and coordinate each rally.
- Put your heads together and identify what could be covered at the P.E.P. rallies. Please list below and discuss with your group.

- _____
  _____

- _____
  _____

- _____
  _____

- _____
  _____

Section Four-

The *One-On-One Career Mentoring and Performance Facilitation Program*

Review the Three Stages of One-On-One
Career Mentoring and Performance Facilitation Program

If team unit leaders want to be effective at helping their direct reports be the best at their position so the team unit is best in its functional area and the organization best in its industry, they need to learn how to execute the three stages of *The One-On-One Career Mentoring and Performance Facilitation* Program .

Many team leaders want to start and remain in Stage Three, the action stage. Unit leaders are not use to starting in *Stage One* (engaging, building rapport and a sharing relationship) and then moving to *Stage Two* (understanding and planning) and then to *Stage Three* (action and results) because it takes effort and time.

The three stages of the *One-On-One Program* are outlined on next page. We will discuss the dimensions in each of the three stages separately and tie them together.

The Three Stages of the Career & Performance Process		
Stage One **Slow Pace**	**Stage Two** **Moderate Pace**	**Stage Three** **Very Fast Pace**
Building A Working and **Sharing Relationship**	***Dialogue, Understanding*** ***and Establishing a Plan***	**Executing the Plan and** **Achieving Results**
• A Common Ground	• Δ **Team Leadership** **Model-***Challenges*	• **Gap Closure** **System- The** **4 M's**
• Trust	• **Gap Closure** *System*-**Objectives**	• **One-on-One** **Meetings**
• Empathy	• **Gap Closure** **System -***Tasks*	• **Positive** **Reinforcement**
• Respect	• **Task Expert** **Process-**	• **Constructive** **Confrontation**

Listening

Attending   **Responding**

The Three Helping Communication Skills

161

Stage One-Building a Working and Sharing Relationship

To be a skilled helper and performance facilitator, a team leader needs to continually build and maintain a working and sharing relationship with direct reports. Team leaders know that building a cohesive team is important, especially after you move into a highly competitive situation that requires team play. The stronger the bond, the better the team will work together to achieve the objective(s). We will now discuss the four dimensions in *Stage One* that you the team leader needs to establish in One-On-One meetings to help build strong working relationships:

- A Common Bond
- Trust
- Empathy
- Respect

A Common Bond

The workforce of America is becoming more diverse each day. The challenge of the organization is to build a common bond that will bring everyone together. This *Model* supports the idea of developing a cause, "Being the Best in Our Field" that will excite and unite everyone in the company. Once this common bond is established, barriers will be broken, people will focus on meeting the "Best in Our Field Objectives" .

The common bond between employees at work should include: a) viewing

diversity as a strength, b) meeting the needs of customers, shareholders, fellow employees and family members, c) achieving the department, division and organization objectives to become "Best in Our Industry", d) becoming a team builder, e) becoming a performance facilitator to help each other grow personally and professionally, f) making work a springboard to purpose, success and happiness as one reaches out to help those in one's circle of life, and g) helping fellow team members become a leader (the best) in their field so it enhances and advances everyone's career.

In essence, the more you have in common with another individual, the closer you feel to that person no matter what the differences might be. There is an old saying "birds of a feather flock together". You just have to make sure you come up with the same feathers (identifying the one or many things that bond you together).

Trust

In an age of intense competition, "mutual suspicion" has in many cases replaced "mutual" and "reciprocal" trust. Still, mutual and reciprocal trust is the basic ingredient for all honest and effective human relationships. The employer and employee, the customer and salesperson, and members of the same team must be bonded by mutual trust and reciprocal trust or the relationship will not grow.

Mutual trust

People <u>believe</u> in each other. If you are to achieve this relationship with others, then it must begin with you.

1) Mutual trust starts with <u>total honesty</u>, even at your expense. There should be no exaggeration, no cover ups, no distortion and no white lies. It is a contagious characteristic that will spread to others.
2) <u>Admit your mistakes</u>. If you know the other person will admit being wrong, you feel more secure in that relationship.
3) <u>Be sincere</u> when you relate to others. Sincerity instills confidence and builds rapport.
4) Put mutual trust <u>above your own ambition and ego</u>. Suspicion, doubt and envy must be set aside.

Reciprocal Trust

People <u>accept help</u> from those they trust. When the relationship is one of acceptance and trust, offers of help are appreciated, listened to, seen as potentially helpful and often acted upon. An individual accepts help from someone whose perceived motives are congenial to him. When one feel his worth as a person is valued, he is able to place himself in psychological readiness to receive help.

A team unit leader can continually measure trust by asking direct reports where they are on the trust scale with each other and with their unit leader. The scale can be 1 to 10 with 10 being high and 1 low. It is important to aim at keeping the mean score of the team unit at 8 and above. You, the team unit leader, can periodically assess where all the team members are on the trust scale by asking them to give you a number on the trust scale. The rating scale numbers can be collected without names on them. The unit leader can determine a mean score on himself/herself and the members and develop a plan to increase trust.

Empathy

Empathy is the key condition in developing close relationships and helpful communication with another person. Not only must another person's feelings be understood, but this understanding must be put into words to that individual.

The *first step* in communicating with empathy is to listen carefully to what an individual is saying about how they feel as a result of what is happening to them. The *second step* is thinking of words that represent the person's feelings and situation. The *third step* is to respond using the words that accurately describe how the individual is feeling.

Empathy and sympathy are different. An expression of sympathy usually tells the person you are sorry about their situation or what has happened to them. It communicates: "I feel bad for you." You have to be careful with sympathy statements because the receiver might interpret your message as saying "I feel sorry for you". This type of statement can make a person angry because they don't want anyone to feel sorry for them. An empathetic statement shows more respect to the person than a sympathetic statement.

When we respond with empathy, we show that we understand what someone is truly feeling. Some people try to take a shortcut and say, "I know what you mean," or "I hear you." Those types of phrases are used because people might not really know how a person is really feeling and it is an easy statement to make. To really help someone understand their feeling, you have to put a label on the feeling.

The helpfulness of empathic responding knows no bounds. The more you can label the feelings of a person in an accurate way, the more a person feels you understand them. It can build meaningful relationships and most of all it is a way to take a person from an angry or bitter state to one that is natural and positive. It provides an opportunity for a person to work through anger, fear, and hurt and move into a logical state of mind where they can make wise decisions and be more productive.

How many bad decisions have people made at work because they were angry or mad at someone. When a person makes important decisions, he/she should be in a logical state of mind and not one of anger. Team leaders and team members can help fellow employees stay positive and make wise decisions.

Respect

Respect is another key condition to being an effective *Helper* and *Performance Facilitator*. Respect is the belief we have in another person's worth and potential. We demonstrate respect by good attending behavior and showing our confidence in another person's ability to solve his/her own problems. We do this by supporting their efforts rather than doing things for them.

It means communicating as one adult to another and not acting as parents telling their children what to do. To show respect to a person, you should be non-judgmental and have unconditional/positive regard for the person, even if he fails once or twice. The person's effort and ability to perform tasks play a part in how we view one another. There are five communication styles or roles people play below that show disrespect to individuals. These styles show disrespect because they don't help the individual solve his or her own situation or problem.

#1-The detective role – This individual is eager to track down the facts of the situation and grills you about the details of what happened. The detective controls the flow of the conversation and puts people on the defensive.

#2-The magician role – This individual makes the problem you have described disappear just like they would make a bunny disappear in a hat. The magician says the problem will eventually take care of itself so there is no need to discuss it.

#3-The foreman role – The foreman, who is pushing for productivity, believes if you are kept busy you want think about the problem. It is telling you that completing the assigned task is more important than your problem. In essence, hard work will make you forget about your problem.

#4-The swami role – The swami guesses and predicts exactly what is going to happen. By declaring the forecast, you are relieved of responsibility and you can sit back and let the prophecy come true. This person knows everything.

#5-The sign painter role – The sign painter thinks your problem can be solved by putting a name on it. The sign painter has an unlimited inventory of labels to affix to a person and their problem. This person attempts to identify the problem but not help you solve it.

Stage Two-Dialogue, Understanding and Establishing a Plan

The four dimensions of the *Second Stage* include:

- The Δ Team Leadership Model: Being the Best
- The Gap Closure Model: Establishing Objectives to Be Best
- The Gap Closure Model: Identifying the Tasks that will Meet the Objectives (Close the Gap from where you Start and End)
- The Task Expert Process-Building Expert Leaders in their Field

The Δ Team Leadership Model: Being the Best By Meeting Objectives

The Δ **Team Leadership Model: Being the Best by Meeting Objectives** is a leadership development and performance management system that can help team unit leaders transform their direct reports into leaders in their field and the unit into the best in its functional area. The team leader and members need to identify the challenge(s) and then establishes objectives that if met would meet the challenge(s). If the objectives are clear, believable, achievable and monitored closely, the *objectives* and challenges will be met. When looking at the Triangle, the team unit leader is placed at the bottom of the triangle which signifies the support for the team. The unit is stationed on the left side of the triangle and the team members are on the right side. The words "Becoming Leaders in Our Field" are on the inside of the Triangle. During the One-On-One sessions, the unit leaders will help direct reports manage personal issues and focus on completing their assigned tasks to meet their objectives and the unit's objectives. If everyone meets individual objectives, they can then be called *Best in Their Field*.

Challenges (meeting objectives) are what an organization, division, department and individual face on a day-to-day basis. Some challenges are more serious than others. As a skilled helper/performance facilitator, we need to be sensitive and know when the problem or challenge is critical and needs more time to be discussed. If we know the issue is important, then we should take the time to be attentive, listen and respond to help individuals or the group develop action tasks to meet the challenge at that time.

If it is a deep personal problem that someone is experiencing and you don't have the time at that point in the day to be attentive, defer the issue to a point during the day or suggest they go to the employment assistance program (E.A.P.) to discuss the situation. .

The Gap Closure System-Establishing Objectives to Meet Challenges
Copyright © 2018 Michael V. Mulligan

The *Gap Closure System* is an approach that helps individuals and team units understand where they are today and where they need to be tomorrow in order to meet challenge(s) and be successful. Individuals and groups analyze their challenges and then establish objectives that need to be met. Some example objectives would include:

1) We need to increase our truck sales from $5 billion to $6 billion dollars starting January 1, 20_____ and concluding on December 31, _____.
2) We need to reduce our expenses in our department from $2 million to $1.8million starting January 1, _____ and concluding December 31, _____.
3) We need as a team to raise our functioning level as a Performance Facilitator and Helping Communicator from a mean score of 2.0 to 3.0 starting January 1, 20_____ and concluding December 31, 20_____.
4) We need to lose weight in our department from a mean of 210 lbs to a mean of 190 lbs starting January 1, _____ and concluding December 31, _____.
5) We need to raise our customer satisfaction score of 75% to 90% starting January 1, 20_____ and concluding July 1, _____.

The Gap Closure System-Establishing Tasks to Meet Objectives

As you or your team unit establishes an objective that needs to be met to meet a challenge, you then need to identify tasks that need to be executed to help meet the objective or close the Gap. An example of an objective is given below.

- **Objective**- Our team unit will lose weight from a mean *sco*re of 210 lbs (the average weight of 10 people in our department) to a mean score of 190 lbs starting January 1, _____ and concluding December 31, _____
  (*Team Unit Tasks*)
  Task # One- Each person on team needs to lose 20 pounds in 12 months.
  Task # Two- Each person on the team needs to lose 1.75 lbs each month.
  (**Individual Tasks**)
  Task #One -Each member on the team will attend the meetings at weight watchers for one year.
  Task # Two-Each person on team will not have anything to eat after 8pm.

The Task Expert Process (TEP)- A Five Step Process
Copyright © 2018 Michael V. Mulligan

The *Task Expert Process* is a process that unit leaders can use in One-On-One sessions to help their direct reports establish and execute tasks to meet objectives (challenges). This five step program is meant to help individuals execute all their assigned tasks in an expert manner so the gaps in the *Gap Closure System* are closed or the objectives are met by the dates that were established.

In the *first step*, the unit leader and direct reports identify the tasks that need to be met to help achieve a specific objective in the *Gap Closure Model*.

In the *second step*, the direct report and unit leader identifies the tasks where coaching is not needed. Direct report is empowered to do tasks.

In the *third step*, the Team Unit Leader will coach the direct report on the tasks where he/she needs coaching. This is a crucial step because there are a lot of positions today that require on the job training and the team leader or someone else on the team needs to be an expert to teach those tasks necessary to do the job so objectives are met.

In the *fourth step*, the direct report is empowered to perform the remaining tasks.

In the <u>fifth step</u>, the direct report at this time is an expert in performing all the tasks that have been assigned to him/her and should be able to meet his/her objectives and help the unit meet it's objectives. There should be an expert book where people are identified as experts in certain area so they can help others,

The One-On One sessions should help the direct report become an expert at their position and target the next position. Then new tasks can be identified so the direct report can work toward being prepared for the targeted position. This is where career mentoring comes is very helpful..

Stage Three-Executing the Plan and Achieving Results

Once you have identified your objectives and the tasks each direct report needs to achieve to meet the predefined objectives, you will move into *Stage Three*,

Executing the Plan and Achieving Results. The four conditions of *Stage Three* include:

- The Gap Closure System-The Four M's
- One-on-One Meetings
- Constructive Confrontations/Immediacy
- Positive Reinforcement Communication

The Gap Closure System-The Four Ms

As direct reports begin to execute the action plans (tasks) unit leaders will:

— *Monitor* how direct reports are executing their tasks
— *Measure* the direct report's efforts and results
— *Modify* individual tasks based on meeting unit objectives
— *Meet* individual and the unit's objectives (*Close the Gap*).

One-on-One Meetings

Unit leaders will meet with their direct reports and boss once a month discussing the *Four M's*, confronting and providing positive reinforcement to each other. The One-On-One sessions will keep everyone focused on what needs to be accomplished to meet the objectives and *Close the Gaps*.

The One- On- One meetings will help unit leaders manage their direct reports more effectively. If a direct report has a personal issue at home or with a fellow worker, you can discuss the situation One-On-One with him/her. If two direct reports are going after each other in a harmful way during team meetings, you can talk to each of them alone and point out that their behavior is destructive to the good of the team as well as their working relationship. It is difficult to solve these type of problems during a team meeting. You always want to save face for each individual.

Copyright © 2018 Michael V. Mulligan

Constructive Confrontation/Immediacy

The word "confrontation" is often associated with the stripping away of a person's defenses and brutally exposing his or her weaknesses. The *One-On- One Model* advocates a constructive confrontation. It is not punitive and cruel. Constructive or performance facilitating confrontation helps the individual examine the inconsistencies in his/her work/life and to make better use of personal strengths and resources.

The focus is on appropriate behavior and not the person. Confrontation without an established working relationship is rarely helpful. The model emphasizes that you must earn the right to confront and this is done through building relationships. This is why we say team unit leaders need to start in *Stage One* of the *Performance Facilitation Process* and move to *Stage Three* after strong relationships have been formed. Confrontation can be damaging creating high levels of anxiety in a person.

Immediacy represents the working relationships you have at the moment with an individual. If you have a good working relationship, it is easier to use constructive confrontation to point out discrepancies between what a person says he/she is going to do and what he/she actually does.

Positive Reinforcement Communication

Just as it is important to point out discrepancies in performance, it is important to recognize excellent work and provide positive feedback on a timely basis. When an individual completes a task or project, meets predetermined objectives or behaves in a certain way to facilitate performance in others, the person should be complimented or recognized. Positive reinforcement should be done on an intermittent basis. This means people should be rewarded or praised at different times without expecting it. If we reward or praise someone all the time, it doesn't mean as much. The problem is that people aren't praised or recognized enough and especially at the right times.

The Three Helping Communication Skills

To function at a helpful level, one needs to master the following three Helping *Communication Skills* which include:

- **Attending Skills**

- **Focus Listening Skills**

- **Accurate Responding Skills**

Attending Skills

Attending skills represent the non-verbal behavior or physical gestures you reflect while listening to another speak. These behaviors, such as facial expressions, eye contact, mannerisms, movement and posture carry messages to persons with whom you talk. Your physical responses reflect your interest in others, respect and how much you care for them. Your attending skills can send the message to others that you care for them as a person.

Attending skills include non-verbal communication, body language and warmth. Non-verbal communication represents at least 70% of the communication between people. If your physical gestures show interest in what other individuals are saying in One-On-One and team meetings, it will make everyone on the team feel important and will reinforce sharing. If your eyes are elsewhere when someone is speaking or you are texting, it makes the person feel what he/she is saying is not that important. This shows disrespect to the individual.

The five attending skills that you need to focus on include your:

- Facial expressions
- Eye contact
- Mannerisms and gestures
- Space
- Posture

Copyright © 2018 Michael V. Mulligan

Focus Listening Skills

Focus listening takes a lot of energy and commitment and is very difficult for most people to do. Some of the reasons we are not good listeners are:

1. We are pre-occupied in thought. We might be thinking of the project or task we have to get done by 5 p.m. We also could be thinking of something that happened a few hours ago that was distressing and we can't get it out of our minds. There are many things that can distract us.

2. We are thinking about what we are going to say and not concentrating on what others are communicating. If we feel that we are going to be evaluated every time we say something in a meeting, we most likely will concentrate on what we are going to say rather than listening to others.

3. We might not care for the person talking or the subject matter being discussed. If we dislike or are prejudiced toward a person, we are less likely to listen to what that individual has to say. In addition, if we don't care much about the subject being discussed, we can easily tune out.

4. We don't know what to concentrate on when a person is talking to us. A focused listener should concentrate on two areas.
   - Understanding the person's feelings and mood based on his/her words and tone of voice.
   - Understanding the person's message or what he/she is really saying.

We use the terminology *focused listening*, because one has to really concentrate on what a person is saying if he/she is to truly understand the individual's message and feelings.

The problem is that an individual needs to clear everything out of their head and prepare themselves to be a good listener. Dr. Michael Mulligan, a former catcher in baseball, gives the example of pitching to the catcher. When the pitcher gets ready to throw his next pitch, the catcher has to be i prepared to catch the pitch. If the catcher is not concentrating on the type and the speed of the pitch, the ball could hit the catcher some place other than the mitt. One has to concentrate and be ready if the ball/message is to be received cleanly/clearly.

Accurate Responding Communication Skills

To be a highly skilled helping communicator, it is important that your response hits the target so it helps to increase understanding. If you are discussing a particular problem with your doctor and the doctor doesn't respond accurately to what you said to clarify what the problem is at this time, the wrong medication can be relayed to the pharmacist. The medication or action prescribed can cause great damage to that person if the prescription is wrong.

Most people are ineffective at accurately responding. They don't listen long enough to gain a clear picture of the problem, and their response will generally miss the target. This is where a person can take the conversation of someone in another direction. However, the person speaking should learn how to keep their remarks to the point, and not ramble. This can help the listener. A long speech can cause another person's mind to fall asleep after three minutes. You should try to promote ongoing interaction between you and others. The sound of one's own voice wakes the mind up and keeps you alert.

Accurate responding communication is listening to what a person is saying and feeding back what has been said in a descriptive manner. This enhances the understanding of the situation or problem. If we communicate accurately, we increase understanding. If our communication misses the target, we decrease understanding and this can impact the decision making process in a negative way.

Three important factors in accurate responding include:

1) Not interrupting others but truly listening to their message and feelings.
2) Broadening your vocabulary with feeling words so you can respond with words that accurately describes one's feelings and situations.
3) Working on the tone and loudness of your voice, so you can send the "appropriate" message.

If you want yourself and others to go through a training program to become a more effective *Helping Communicator* and *Performance Facilitator,* please call Mulligan and Associates Inc. at 847 981-5725

Copyright © 2018 Michael V. Mulligan

Task Two-

Assess Self as a *Helper & Performance Facilitator*

The Helper/Performance Facilitator's Communication Survey

Please answer the following 25 statements using the following scale

1-Never   2-Seldom   3-Sometimes   4-Usually   5-Always

1. When someone is talking directly to me or to our group, my   1 2 3 4 5
    eye contact, facial expressions and posture sends the message
    I am interested in what that person has to say.

2. I acknowledge people's presence by saying hello and calling   1 2 3 4 5
    them by their appropriate name.

3. I focus listen so distractions don't get in the way of my   1 2 3 4 5
    identifying the feelings and messages that a person is sending.

4. I target respond to help others better understand their situation   1 2 3 4 5
    so they can develop their ideas, make decisions and solve
    problems.

5. When individuals are in an unpleasant mood, I respond with   1 2 3 4 5
    empathy, labeling what they are feeling so they can work
    through issues, problems and any anger they are feeling.

6. My non-verbal and verbal communication style reflects my   1 2 3 4 5
    respect for others and shows that I believe in their ability to
    solve their own problems

7. I work hard developing a trust base and common ground   1 2 3 4 5
    between others and myself.

8. I am careful about taking time away from others but know   1 2 3 4 5
    when it is appropriate to do so.

9. I work closely with my manager/direct reports to develop and   1 2 3 4 5
    achieve objectives that helps my department and organization
    meet their plan.

10. I put objectives, plans and status reports into writing and   1 2 3 4 5
    circulate them to inform people.

11. I work closely with my direct reports using a the *Task Expert*   1 2 3 4 5
    Program to help them become best in their field.

12. I meet with my manager/direct report monthly, one-on-one to evaluate my/his contribution to the department's objectives and discuss how I/he can improve and help the team.   1 2 3 4 5

13. I meet with my manager/direct reports a minimum of once a month to discuss the objectives in the business plan assessing expectations are met.   1 2 3 4 5

14. I attend with my manager and colleagues the team meetings monthly and implement the tasks that need to be done to be successful.   1 2 3 4 5

15. I work with my direct reports to build a career path profile so they can better direct, manage and market their career journey.   1 2 3 4 5

16. I always do what I say I will do. I walk my talk.   1 2 3 4 5

17. I maintain a positive attitude and create excitement, enthusiasm and energy in others.   1 2 3 4 5

18. I have a positive attitude during the day and keep a sense of humor to keep things in perspective.   1 2 3 4 5

19. I spot talent and strengths in others and encourage them to use it.   1 2 3 4 5

20. I am a team maker promoting performance facilitating partnerships and partners helping partners to grow personally and professionally.   1 2 3 4 5

21. I communicate with others so everyone knows what is expected, what has been done and what needs to be done.   1 2 3 4 5

22. I praise, give credit where credit is due and show appreciation to others based on what they accomplish.   1 2 3 4 5

23. I provide feedback to others, both positive and negative, in a tactful manner and on a continuous basis.   1 2 3 4 5

23. I constructively confront others when it is necessary to point out discrepancies so everyone is back on the same page.   1 2 3 4 5

25. I think before I speak so I don't put others on the defensive.   1 2 3 4 5

TOTAL SCORE_____   **MEAN SCORE** _____

Discussion Questions

1. Which three statements of the 25 do you consider to be your greatest strengths? List the numbers of these statements below. Why did you select these statements?

_____

_____

_____

2. Which three statements do you consider to be areas you need to strengthen? List the numbers of these statements below. Why did you select these statements?

_____

_____

_____

3. Which three statements do you think people need to master the most to be helpful to others? List the numbers of the statements below. Why did you select these statements?

_____

_____

_____

**Define Career Mentor, Learn the *Route 56*
Career Management Model and Take *Career
Management Survey and Review Results***

Defining a Career Mentor

In the case of our *Triangle Team Leader Model*, we define a *Career Mentor* as a helper, performance facilitator and idiosyncratic coach, a manager who helps their direct reports become a task expert at their position so they are called best in their field. The mentor also helps the direct report target their next position and prepare for it. This means using the *Task Expert Process* identifying tasks where the person needs more coaching. The *Career Mentor* works with the direct report for two to five years or longer. He/she finds specialist mentors who are experts at performing certain tasks to teach how to perform the tasks he/she cannot teach the direct reports.

To summarize, the goals of a *Career Mentor* in a work environment include:

1) Helping direct reports become an expert at performing specific tasks related to their position so they meet the objectives that makes them the best at their position, the team unit best in its functional area and the organization best in its industry.
2) Helping direct reports learn more about himself/herself so they can target the next position and prepare for it
3) Help direct report learn the Route 56 Career Management Model so they learn how to plan and manage a successful career journey.
4) Help direct reports increase their knowledge about the six career modules that make up the *Route 56 Career Management Model* by taking The *Career Management Survey* located on the following websites- www.mulliganassoc.com and www.managemycareer.info and reviewing the results with the manager on the CMQ score card

Learn the *Route 56 Career Management Model* Which Can Help Individuals Manage Their Career from Now to Retirement

The *Route 56 Career Management Model* was created to help individuals chart and manage their career journey. The *first 5* in the Model means you should plan your career out no more than five years at a time. You should develop a yearly growth plan and if properly executed, you should not be the same person in 5 years that you are today.

You live to grow and you grow by acquiring experience, knowledge, degrees, credentials and skills. This growth can place us in positions that we never thought we could occupy when in high school, college and while in our 20's and 30's. For example, Barack Obama probably never dreamed of being President of the United States but by obtaining his law degree from Harvard and being elected as a United States Senator, it gave him the opportunity to be elected President.

This means if you develop and execute a yearly career pathing and growth plan looking five years ahead, you will develop plans that can eventually put you in a career position that you never dreamed you could obtain. Abraham Maslow's self actualization theory states man wants to become and be.

(Example Rolling Five Year Ongoing Plans-But Not Necessarily like Below)

13 to 18	19 to 23	24 to 28	29 to 33	34 to 38	39 to 43	44 to 48	49 to 53	54 to 58	59 to 63+

The *6* represents six career management modules that you should be focusing each year as you move forward in your career. You set a growth objective for each of the five modules listed below and develop action plans to meet each objective.

1. Career Transitioning

- Moving through five growth stages- starting, advancement, peaking, uncertainty and semi-retirement or moving through this cycle two or three times due to career change
- Working in more than 10 to 15 jobs and for more than five organizations
- Learning how to deal with change
- Being an Expert Task Performer or Best in Your Field in your present position
- Continuously charting your career or being unemployed for a long time

2.Career Selection (Choosing the next career field and position that's right for you)

- Self Assessment – develop a *Career Profile*
- Career Assessment – explore the world of work-industries and positions?
- Select an industry and positions that match your *Career Profile.*

3..Career Preparation (Qualify yourself for your targeted career field and position)

- Select and attend the right college or university
- Take courses in college that prepare you for chosen career field/ position(s)
- Internships in career fields, co-op work, or part-time work
- College graduation – A.A., A.S., B.A., B.S.
- Graduate work, degrees and being certified in your field
- On the Job Training-workshops, seminars, certification
- Find a career mentor- someone who can help you grow and be successful

4. Career Placement (Job Search – Place yourself in your next targeted position)

- Target career field and position
- Write your resume and marketing letters based on your targeted position
- Develop a job search sales and marketing plan
  (Networking, websites, direct mail, recruiters, support groups, job fairs)
- Sharpen your interviewing and telephone skills
- Develop your negotiating skills
- Meet with hiring managers and executives and obtain an offer
- Negotiate your offer
- Integrate yourself into the company/organizations
- Excel as a leader

5. Career Advancement (Becoming what you want to be)

- Graduate from high school
- Graduate from a college or university
- Finish graduate/professional school
- Start and move up the leadership and management ladder
- Know the key factors to advancement
- Obtain and work with a career mentor or executive coach
- Build and be on high performance teams
- Continually build your credentials
- Develop and stay in touch with a network of leaders
- Learn how to wave your flag
- Continually execute the *Route 56 Career Management Model*
- Know when you have peaked in your career field and position

6. Career Fulfillment (Meeting your needs and becoming the best in your field)

- Meet your needs at work (survival, security, social needs, self-esteem)
- Assess your work satisfaction and develop a plan to enjoy your work
- Balance your life and work in order to get the most out of your life
- Become and be the best in your field – an expert leader
- Continually fill out the Route 66 Career Satisfaction Survey so you can place yourself on the right career route-the right fit and rewards

You should be aware of the *Five Career Growth Stages* most people experience. When planning and evaluating our career journey, many of us do not know where we should be in our career at a certain age. We have developed the following chart to illustrate where the average worker should be in their career growth at a certain age in their life. The illustration below shows the *Five Career Growth Stages* a normal person would take as he/she works for a number of organizations and companies and moves slowly up the career ladder. An exception would be the individual on a fast track with a company or one who start or buys a company early in his/her life, grows the company and sells it for a lot of money. Even though that person is financially secure, he/she can be in the uncertainty stage. What do I do next? Or the semi-retirement stage where you travel and help others in the world without a monetary gain. If you start a new career, it puts you back in the first stage of the cycle, the career starting stage.

Age Passages	Five Career Growth Stages
13 to 18	
19 to 23	The Career Starting Stage
24 to 28	
29 to 33	
34 to 38	The Career Advancement Stage
39 to 43	
44 to 48	
49 to 53	The Career Peaking Stage
54 to 58	
59 to 63	The Career Uncertainty Stage
64 Plus	The Career Semi-Retirement Stage

We will describe these stages in more detail on the following pages.

The **Career Starting Stage** generally includes 13 to 28 year olds. These individuals are trying to figure out where they are today, where they want to be tomorrow and how they are going to get there. They are trying to decide what career field to enter, what positions best fits them and how to prepare for their career field and position(s). They also want to know how to conduct a job search to obtain their desired career positions after graduation from college. Many parents allow their son or daughter to live at home while in their 20's which enables them to zigzag through a number of career fields to learn what they should eventually pursue. However, you might see individuals of all ages today in Stage One a number of times as they switch careers and start over to find new employment. ©

The **Career Advancement Stage** generally includes those individuals 29 to 43 years of age. These individuals want to be empowered and have more responsibility in their present job. They also want to be promoted in title when they think they are ready and be placed in positions that offer more status, power and pay. This group is continually asking themselves the following questions:

- Do I need an MBA, advanced degree, special credentials or certification to advance?
- Can I have a company senior executive mentor and meet with him or her frequently?
- Can I meet the performance expectations of my boss? Do I do have enough resources to be successful?
- Am I perceived as a high-potential and talented person by my boss and others in the company?
- Are my personal, professional and financial needs being met by my present company?
- Do I have a better chance of advancing my career by staying or leaving?

The majority of those in the career advancement group are now married, have children, own a house, and are starting to save for their children's college education. These individuals might have more going on in their lives than they can handle.

The **Career Peaking Stage** generally includes individuals 44 to 58 years of age. These employees are the team leaders, managers and expert specialists in the organization. They are the visionaries, strategists, the planners, and the ones that establish the company's culture and receive the highest compensation.

During this 14-year period, individuals will advance until they reach the highest level of competency. Employees who want to keep advancing must know when they have reached the top in their career path. People who take on jobs they cannot handle eventually find themselves in trouble and could possibly be fired. It is nice to see yourself as superman or superwoman, but you also must be realistic in taking on new positions or walking into situations where you cannot be successful. This stage calls for honest career decision making. On the other hand, many people are afraid to take risks and stay in positions that offer very little challenge.

The **Career Uncertainty Stage** generally includes those 58 to 63 years of age. The reason this phase is called the Career Uncertainty Phase is because schools, organizations and companies usually want this age group to leave or retire early to reduce costs. The individuals in this category usually know they are on thin ice. This group costs the company more in benefits and total compensation than any other group. Because these individuals can start taking money from their pension funds at 59 ½, it is tempting for many to leave their companies or organizations early. The problem is having health insurance coverage until one is 65 and not spending your savings too early in life. Unless individuals in this age group own a business, occupy a professional position (MD., Dentist, Lawyer, etc.) or have a special skill a company really needs, they are vulnerable. Each person in this group should have a transition plan in place and execute the plan when it is the right time to leave. If a person in this group can start their own business and succeed, they could work longer.

The **Career Semi-Retirement Stage** generally includes those individuals 64 and over. People in this group still want to work for pay but not 50 to 70 hours per week. They would like to work 20 to 30 hours per week and have free time to travel and be with family and friends. This group wants to keep working to challenge their minds, use their talent, supplement their income and feel like they are contributing to society. Individuals in the *Uncertainty and Semi-Retirement Stages* should look at their avocations or passions (hobbies, special interests, etc.) and build a small business from their avocations. They might also think of doing team teaching in a junior, senior high school or community college, or be a part-time executive coach and mentor for employees in their former company. ©

The exceptions are those individuals who change careers two or three times in their lives. They will probably go through all five-growth phases in each career. For example, a person who starts a business at 28 and then sells it for 10 million dollars at age 35 would have gone through all five career growth stages. Another example would include a person starting as a school teacher, leaving education to work for a corporation and then starting and managing his or her own company. Can you think of other people who have gone through the five career stages early in life and are now in the career starting stage again?

Take Career Management Survey

You should take the *Career Management Competency Survey* at www.mulliganassoc.com and review your E-mail score report . We ask you to review the information to the statements on your *Career Management Survey Score Report* that was e-mailed to you. You answered each statement by marking:

➤ *a strong need to know the subject*
➤ *a moderate need to know the subject*
➤ *no need to know the subject*
➤ *an expert (know subject)*

Once you have your e-mail CMS score report is in hand, go to the statements you had a moderate or strong need to know. You can click on the statement from the e-mail score report and read the information or take an assessment. The goal is for you to be familiar with all statements on the *Career Management Survey* and the following podcasts. Some information on the survey and podcasts relate to attending college. You might have some direct reports who would like to obtain an A.A., B.A. M.B.A. or Ph.D.

<u>Podcast # 1</u> - **Charting Your Career Path &Managing Your Career Path until Retirement.**

<u>Podcast # 2</u> - **Selecting the Industry / Positions That are Best for You and Will Put and Keep You on the Right Career Path**

<u>Podcast # 3</u> - **Preparing for the ACT and SAT and Understanding Your Score Reports as They Relate to College Academic Readiness, Admissions Selectivity, Career/Major Selection, Financial Scholarships and Course Placement**

<u>Podcast # 4</u> - **Developing a College Selection Profile and Selecting and Enrolling in the College/University That Fits You.**

<u>Podcast # 5</u> - **Obtaining an A.A., B.A. or B.S. College Degree on Your Timeline and Graduating with a Good Job.**

<u>Podcast # 6</u> - **Working with Your Boss to Chart Your Career Path, Become an Expert in Your Position, and Obtain More Experience to Advance**

<u>Podcast # 7</u> - **Identifying and Working with Mentors that will Help You Chart and Manage a Successful Career Journey**

Podcast # 8 - Obtaining the Right Graduate or Professional Degree and Being Active in Your Profession to Advance

Podcast # 9 - Obtaining Personal Fulfillment from Work

Podcast # 10 - Defining Leadership and Management, Assessing Your Strengths as a Unit Leader and Manager and Charting Your Career Path in Management or Non-Management

Podcast # 11 - Developing and Executing a Work- for-Pay Career Plan from Age 50 until Retirement

Podcast # 12 - Knowing What to Do When You Lose Your Job.

Podcast # 13 - Executing a Job Acquisition Process to Find a New Position in Your Present Organization or When Unemployed

Podcast #14 - Operating as a Career Path Mentor

The information in the statements on the survey and on Podcast will be updated each year.

Task Four-

Know Your Direct Reports and Help Them Grow

Gathering Information on Direct Reports-
These Sheets Can Be Reproduced

NAME OF DIRECT REPORT
_____

NICKNAME:
_____

BIRTH PLACE AND DATE:
_____

FAMILY SITUATION
_____

SPOUSE – NAME AND OCCUPATION:
_____
CHILDREN – NAME(S), AGE(S) AND INFORMATION
_____

_____

ABOUT THE DIRECT REPORT

WHERE BORN?
_____

WHERE DID HE/ SHE GROW UP
_____

WHAT DOE REPORT LIKE TO DO WHEN NOT WORKING?:
_____

WHAT IS CAREER ASPIRATION OF DIRECT REPORT?
_____

REPORT EVALUATES CAPABILITY TO PERFORM CERTAIN TASKS-
_____

STRENGTHS:
_____

_____

_____

WEAKNESSES
_____

_____

IN WHICH AREAS CAN THE COMPANY HELP THE REPORT NOW?

DIRECT REPORT SHARES HIGH SCHOOL AND COLLEGE INFORMATION

INDICATE HIGHEST DEGREE COMPLETED

HIGH SCHOOL: FR   SOPH   JR   SR

COLLEGE: FR   SOPH   JR   SR

VOCATIONAL SCHOOL: CERTIFICATION: _____

GRADUATE SCHOOL: DEGREE RECEIVED: _____

	HIGH SCHOOL	COLLEGE	COLLEGE	COLLEGE
NAME OF SCHOOL AND LOCATION:				
DATES OF ATTENDANCE:				
TYPE OF STUDENT				
COLLEGE MAJOR/ MINOR STUDIES				
FAVORITE SUBJECT(S):				
OFFICES HELD,,EXTRA ACTIVITIES				
HONORS AND AWARDS				

PROFESSIONAL CERTIFICATIONS:

_____

FUTURE TARGETED DEGREE AND TRAINING:

_____

Direct Report Shares Past Career Path and Evaluates His or Her Performance in the Last Position

Please list below the companies/organizations that hired you, the dates you worked with each organization, and the positions/jobs that you held.

#	Companies or Organizations	Industry	Dates Employed	Positions/Jobs held
1				
2				
3				
4				
5				
6				

What career field or position(s) have these work experiences prepared you to do next?

_____

_____

Have Direct Report Take Career Management Survey

We recommend direct reports take the *Career Management Survey* at www.mulliganassoc.com. Once they receive their score report and review it alone, they should meet with you and go over their answers using the *CMQ Report* below. You want to check off the statements that they know. You can then review the information on the statements where they want to know more. Check off the statements when you think the direct report is knowledgeable about that topic. Your goal is to check off all statements.

Goal -Increase Direct Reports CMQ (Career Management Knowledge)
Review direct reports E-mail Score report and check off statements
where they know or have no need to know. Discuss the Topics where
they have a need to know. You want them to know something about all 60
statements but especially the information they need to know today.

Module 1: Career/Position Transitioning-

1) I need to know why it is important to chart and manage my career journey until retirement.

2) I need to know the five career growth stages of an individual's career journey and identify the growth stage that I am in today.

3) I need to know about the Route 56 Career Management Model that can help me plan and manage my career from where I am today until I retire.

4) I need to know key strategies that can help me manage a successful career journey.

5) I need to know the major challenge I must meet to have a successful career journey.

6) I need to assess if I am satisfied with my present college/university situation and make adjustments.

7) I need to know the challenges that students must meet to be successful in college and graduate professional school.

8) I need to know the challenges that employees must meet to be successful in their present position and organization.

9) I need to know the challenges employees 55 and over must meet to stay employed until they decide to retire.

10) I need to know how to manage being released from my job-Due to acquisitions, downsizing, financial reasons, mergers, restructuring or right sizing .

Module 2: Career/Position Selection

11) I need to know more about charting a career path and the world of work: career fields (industries) and career positions (functional areas). Also check out o'net online for information

12) I need to know the differences between the various work sectors.

13) I need to know the college majors offered and the career fields and career positions that relate to these programs.

14) I need to know more about the franchise world and starting own business.

15) I need to know where the future jobs are going to be.

16) I need to know my ultimate career aspiration at this time and why?

17) I need to know my academic strengths and weaknesses which will help me with educational and career planning.

18) I need to know my interests and preference to perform certain work tasks.

19) I need to know my personal and work values. (What is important to me?).

20) I need to know the work rewards I want in my present or next position.

21) I need to know my skills, what I can do well.

22) I need to know my personality and how specific traits relate to playing leadership roles and being successful at work.

23) I need to know more about myself as an entrepreneur.

24) I need to know more about myself as a consultant.

25) I need to know myself and target a career field and a position that fits me.

Module 3: Career/Position Preparation

26) I need to know how to conduct research and informational interviews to learn the qualifications needed to be hired in ones targeted career position.

27) I need to know the educational programs in high school that will best prepare family members for college, a scholarship and a career.

28) I need to know how to assess myself as a self manager, identify where I need to improve and execute a growth plan.

29) I need to know how to select and enroll in the educational institutions that will best prepare me for my present career field/position or a new position and career field. (trade school, community college, four year college or university or graduate or professional school.

30) I need to know how to obtain money (scholarships, grants, loans and work) to attend college, graduate/ professional school.

31) I need to know why 70% of students attending a community college do not graduate in three years and why 50% of students attending a four year college do not graduate in five

years so a college graduation plan can be developed and achieved.(read the book The Five Goal College Plan)

32) I need to know how to obtain internships, entry level and time line jobs that can provide *On the Job Training and Familiarization* so I can move into a new career/position.

33) I need to know how to work with faculty, academic advisers, and administrators on a college campus to prepare me for my present position or put me on a new career path. (a degree or certification program).

34) I need to know how to become a career manager and help clients, students, family members, and direct reports become a career manager.

35) I need to know where I need to grow in my present position and how. (in-house and professional workshops and programs and using mentors).

Module 4: Career/Position Placement

Review the *Five Goal College Plan* book which discusses finding employment after college)

36) I need to know how to execute *Phase One* of the *Job Acquisition Process,* targeting my next position and developing marketing materials (resumes, marketing letters, job search card, etc.) that will brand me properly so I can obtain interviews and job offers.

37) I need to know how to execute *Phase Two* **of the** *Job Acquisition Process,* implementing the *Five Step Interview Acquisition Plan.*

38) I need to know how to execute *Phase Three* of the *Job Acquisition Process* **sharpening my exploratory, telephone and face to face (high stress) interviewing skills to obtain offers.**

39) I need to know how to execute *Phase Four* of the *Job Acquisition Process*, negotiating a job offer without losing it.

40) I need to know how to execute *Phase Five* of the *Job Acquisition Process*, making a positive start in a new position either in my present company or another company/ organization. (Positive start means building rapport and being accepted by the people who work with and for you - there is no one as smart as all of us)

Module 5: Career/Position Advancement

41) I need to know how to work with my boss to be the best in my position, take on more responsibility and advance my career.

42) I need to know how the professionals define leadership and management.

43) I need to know my competency level to perform specific tasks as a unit leader and manager and then work with my boss and have the opportunity to work with a Specialist Mentor to improve in the identified task areas.

44) I need to know the attributes of a successful CEO or President.

45) I need to know about a leadership development and performance management model that will transform all team members into champion performers and the unit into a championship organization. (A model that can advance units, careers and the total organization).

46) I need to know a *One-On-One Performance Facilitation and Helping Communication Model* that can improve my helping communication with customers, colleagues, direct reports, and friends and family members.

47) I need to know how to measure and raise my emotional intelligence (personal and social competence); a key factor in being a charismatic leader and getting people to follow and work with me.

48) I need to know what derails unit leaders in organizations and what professionals say are the key factors to advancement.

49) I need to know how to assess myself as a performance facilitator and become one in my organization so I can help advance the careers of those I work with every day as well as my own career.

50) I need to know what our unit can do to become *Best in Our Field* and how we can wave our flag to be perceived as *Best in Our Field*

51) I need to know my work culture (race, gender, age of team members and boss) and the group dynamics of my unit/department and take a *Human Relations Survey* and learn what

I can do to improve my relationship with everyone in the department or unit.

52) I need to know and execute the TEAM Program, a process that promotes engagement, the identification of each team member's strengths and asks each team member to use their strengths to meet individual champion and unit championship objectives

53) I need to know and execute a strategic leadership development system that will help our team members develop the objectives of the unit/organization and identify the leadership behaviors necessary to meet the objectives.

54) I need to know how to conduct an effective group/team unit meeting what people share openly and the agenda is covered in a set time limit with goals being met.

55) I need to know how to become a *Career Pathing Mentor* and setup a mentoring program to help clients, family members, and direct reports use their potential to become a top performer and chart and manage a successful career journey.

Module 6: Career/Position Fulfillment

56) I need to know how to create and execute a career management model that will help me enter the right career field and find positions in organizations that will give me fulfillment, satisfaction and happiness in my work.

57) I need to know how to assess whether my basic needs are being met so I can make adjustments and become a top performer.

58) I need to assess my present career situation and make appropriate adjustments.

59) I need to know how to identify my personal and work values and what I want from work so I can strive to honor my values and obtain what I want from work.

60) I need to know how to measure and raise my functioning level as a *Helping Communicator* **so I am more skilled at helping those I interact with at work, home, and in my community. They say fulfillment comes with helping others in a meaningful way.**

Review all 60 statements and be sure direct report are familiar with the information on each statement. Again check off all relevant statements where you think the direct report should be knowledgeable.

The Self Analysis and Career Charting Program

Call Mulligan & Associates at 847 981-5725 if you would like to have direct reports participate in the *Self Analysis and Career Charting Program*. The assessments include:

1. **The Jackson Vocational Interest Blank-** It is an interest assessment which helps a person learn the career areas and college majors that match their interests.
2. **The Mulligan Leadership Personality Profile-**Measures eight personality leadership traits (competitiveness, determination, self directed, organized, patient, helper, innovative and team builder) that are important in being a team unit leader, team member leader and manager. Designed to place people in the right leadership positions and help them develop a growth plan so they can carry out both leadership roles when placed in the situation.
3. **The Leadership and Manager Competency Survey-**Measures a person's competency level to carry out 20 leadership and 40 management tasks. The results can be used in a leadership and management development program.
4. **The 100 Work Tasks Assessment Survey-** This survey helps people identify where they have strengths and where they need coaching.
5. **The MBTI-** A personality assessment that indicates a persons preference to how he becomes energized, makes decisions and operates.
6. **The Interpersonal Communication Assessment Survey -** a survey that measures where a person is functioning when it comes to interacting and helping people understand problems and issues and making appropriate plans to solve their issues and problems.
7. **E.Q. Assessment Survey** a survey that measures one's emotional intelligence – a key ingredient to being a successful leader and human being. Completed by individual and boss if you desire a contrast.
8. **The 21 Personal Values Assessment Survey-** a survey that ranks 21 values of an individual and provides both an individual and team report. If the values of people on a team are too far apart, there could be dissonance on the team with out knowing why.
9. **The Work Values Preference Survey-** A survey that ranks five work values and tells one what an individual values most about work.
10. **The Consultant Assessment Survey*-** helps an individual understand whether or not he or she will enjoy doing consulting work.

Many of these assessments are in this book. You might want to buy a copy for each direct report.

The following is Frederick Herzberg's Motivational Model

What Satisfies Employees

- Fair company policies and procedures
- Effective supervisor
- Positive relationships with supervisors
- Excellent working conditions
- Competitive salaries
- Productive relationships with peers
- Balance between personal life and work
- Excellent relationships with direct reports
- Status
- Security

What Motivates Employees

- Challenge
- Achievement
- Recognition
- Responsibility
- Advancement
- Growth
- Additional Compensation

The Model established by Herzberg should be kept in mind as you get to know each direct report and learn which of the motivators above energizes that person to work harder. Please note the motivator *Challenge* fits our mission statement as *Being Best in Our Field.*

Task Five

Use *the Task Expert Process* to Transform Reports Best at Their Position, the Team Unit Best in Its Functional Area and the Organization Best in its Industry

We recommend you take the following nine steps in executing the *Task Expert Process* with each of your direct reports.

- **Step One-** Understand the Five Phases of Task Expert Process
- **Step Two-** Discuss the vision and mission statements of the organization and gain the direct reports buy in of Being the Best.
- **Step Three-** Review the goals and Best in Field objectives of the organization
- **Step Four-** Review the goals and Best in Field objectives for team unit with each direct report
- **Step Five –** Work with report identifying the objectives they need to meet and the tasks they need to master to meet each objective.
- **Step Six-** Have Direct Report Fill Out and Review *The Skills and Task Competency Survey* to Learn Their Strengths and Weaknesses
- **Step Seven-** Use four M approach (Monitor, Measure, Modify and Meet) to Help Reports achieve Individual and Team Objectives.
- **Step Eight-** Develop an *Expert Task Book* and place the names of the people in the book according to their expertise.
- **Step Nine-** Help all those who performed all the tasks successfully identify their next position and prepare for it. Their title can remain the same but by adding growth tasks their responsibility can grow as well as their pay.

Step One- Understand The Five Phases of The Task Expert Process-

(Phase One)- The team leader identifies the unit objectives that he wants the direct report to help the team meet. Individual objectives are also discussed and written out, Then the team leader and direct report write out the tasks that need to be completed to meet each objective.

(Phase Two)- The team leader and direct report review the list of tasks and the report identifies the tasks he/she can complete and those where they will need some coaching or education. The team leader empowers the report to work on the tasks where he/she is an expert.

(Phase Three)- The direct report identifies the tasks where he/she needs more coaching and education and the team leader becomes a coach or asks someone on the team or elsewhere to coach and educate the report.

This process will be needed more and more in the future as technology changes the way work is done.

(Phase Four) – The direct report becomes willing and able to perform all task necessary to help meet the predetermined objectives.

(Phase Five) - The direct report is now classified an expert performer in completing certain tasks and is placed in the *Task Expert Performer* book.

Step Two- Discuss the vision and mission statements

It is important to discuss the vision and mission statement of the organization with your direct reports because it makes them feel part of the organization. If you are a department head or manager in a large organization that does not have the mission of being the best in our field, you can present the idea to your reports and adopt it as your own mission.

Step Three- Review the suggested goals and objectives of organization

Goal One - Increase Your Income and Cash Flow

Goal Two- Control and Manage Expenses So You Don't Exceed Your Income

Goal Three- Meet the Expectations and Needs of Your Customers and Grow Your Customer Base

Goal Four- Recruit, Develop and Retain Employees Who Will Help You Be The Best in Your Industry

Goal Five- Build a Performance Facilitating Culture, One That Brings Out t he Best In Others To Be Champion Performers-Best in Field

Goal Six- *Meet the Expectations of Your Shareholders*

Goal Seven- *Meet the Expectations and Needs of Your Suppliers*

Goal Eight- *Meet the Needs and Expectations of Family Members*

Goal Nine- *Meet the Expectations and Needs of Retired Employees*

Goal Ten- *Help the Local Community in a Positive Way*

Goal Eleven- *Identify the Strengths of Each Direct Report and Develop a Plan for Them to Use Their Strengths to Achieve the Best in Field Objectives*

Goal Twelve- *Identify the Weaknesses of Each Direct Report and Create a Plan to Transform Them into Strengths*

Goal Thirteen--*Meet Expectations of Colleagues and Fellow Department Heads*

Additional goals

You should go back to page 12 in this manual to review the suggested objectives under each goal.

Step Four- Review the goals and objectives of your team unit

Review pages 147 to 148 in this manual to review what your team unit came up with for team unit goal and objectives. Make changes if necessary and write your team unit goals and objectives below.

Goal One

Objective:

Objective:

Goal Two

Objective

Objective

Goal Three

Objective

Objective

Goal Four

Objective

Objective

Goal Five

Objective

Objective

Your Team Unit Goals and Objectives

Goal Six

Objective

Objective

Goal Seven

Objective

Objective

Goal Eight

Objective

Objective

Goal Nine

Objective

Objective

Goal 10

Objective

Objective

Step Five – Work with direct report identifying the objectives and tasks you want them to complete to meet individual and team unit objectives.

Objective One

Task

Task

Task

Objective Two

Task

Task

Task

Objective Three

Task

Task

Task

Objective Four

Task

Task

Task

Objective Five

Task

Task

Task

Objective Six

Task

Task

Task

Objective Seven

Task

Task

Task

Objective Eight

Task

Task

Task

STEP SIX- REPORTS IDENTIFY THE SKILLS/TASKS IMPORTANT TO MASTER TO MEET DESIGNATED OBJECTIVES AND BE BEST IN POSITION AND THEIR COMPETENCY LEVEL TO EXECUTE THEM

- **REPORTS CIRCLE SKILLS /TASKS ON NEXT PAGES THEY MASTERED**

- **REPORTS LIST SKILLS/TASKS BELOW THAT NEED TO BE MASTERED AND PERFORMED IN PRESENT POSITION**

- **REPORTS CIRCLE THE SKILLS AND TASKS THEY HAVE MASTERED IN THEIR PRESENT POSITION.**
- **REPORTS PUT AN X BY THE SKILLS/TASKS WHERE THEY NEED EDUCATION AND COACHING IN THEIR PRESENT POSITION.**

Abstracting/Conceptualizing
Parts of a system into a whole.
Ideas for surface events.
New spatial relationships.

Administering
A department of people, programs.
A specific activity, such as a test.

Advising
Giving financial counsel, advice.
Advice in an educational system.

Analyzing
Quantitative data, statistical data.
Human/social situations.

Anticipating
Staying one step ahead of moods of the public.
Being able to sense what will be fashionable in consumer goods. .Expecting a problem before it develops, seeing first signs.

Appraising
Evaluating programs or services.
Judging the value of property.
Evaluating performance of individuals.

Arranging
Social functions, events.
Meetings between specific people.

Assembling
Technical apparatus or equipment.
Items of information into a coherent whole.

Auditing
Assessing the financial status of an organization.

Interpreting
Other languages.
Obscure phrases or passages in English.
Meaning of statistical data.

Interviewing
Evaluating applicants to an organization.
Obtaining information from others.

Investigating
Seeking information which individuals may attempt to keep secret. Seeking the underlying causes of a problem.

Laboratory Working
Setting up scientific equipment.
Obtaining results from controlled experiments.

Listening
To extended conversations between others.
To extended conversation from one person.
To recording devices or other listening situations

Locating
Finding people who are missing
Detecting missing information
Sources of help for others

Making Layouts
For printed media
For public displays, posters

Managing
Setting predetermined objectives and working with and through people to achieve the objectives

Mapping
Mapping geographical, physical boundaries and space Putting sequences of events into graphic form.

Budgeting
Outlining costs of a project.
Assuring that money will not be spent in
excess of
funds. Using money efficiently and
economically.

Calculating
Performing mathematical computations.
Assessing risks of an activity in advance.

Classifying
Sorting information into categories.

Coaching
Guiding activities of an athletic team.
Tutoring in academic subjects or other
pursuits on a one-to-one basis.

Collecting
Money or services from people who owe.
Widely scattered items.
Many items in a single class (e. g.
stamps).

Committee Working
Attaining objectives through committee
processes.
Creating and implementing committee
structures.

Measuring
Obtaining accurate scientific
measurements

Mediating
Being a peacemaker between conflicting
parties
Acting as a liaison between competing
interests or differing constituencies

Meeting the Public
Being a receptionist or greeter
Giving tours
Being public representative of an agency
Selling products in a public place
Dealing with public in a service
capacity (e. g.,
policeman or barber)

Moving with Dexterity
Being able to move with speed and
grace (sports, etc.)

Negotiating
Financial contracts - Between
individuals or
groups in conflict

Observing
Physical phenomena with
accuracy - Behavior of human beings
social historical changes
Small details in physical objects - Small
details in written materials

Obtaining Information
From written sources, documents
From unwilling individuals

Compiling
Gathering numerical, statistical data.
Accumulating facts in a given topic area.

Computer Skills
Being aware of the latest technology and how to
use it at work and personally.

Confronting
Obtaining decisions from "reluctant dragons."
Giving bad news to others. Obtaining information
from others who are unwilling to disclose it.
Resolving personal conflicts.

Initiating
Personal contacts with strangers.
New ideas, ways of doing things; new approaches.

Influencing others
Providing service to an individual
Serving a product such as food to individuals

Inspecting
Physical objects to meet standards.
People to determine criteria or detect information.

Outdoor Working
Involvement with the land and its resources
Involvement with animal life
Testing oneself against physical challenges
Involvement with wild animals
Collecting scientific data
Recasting land for commercial use

Operating
Scientific equipment
Mechanical devices, vehicles
Electronic data equipment, computers, etc.

Organizing
Bringing people together for certain tasks
Gathering information and arranging it in clear, interpretable form
Arranging political activity; rousing the public to action

Remembering
Large quantities of information for immediate recall Names, faces, places, etc.
Long sequences of events or instructions

Repairing
Mechanical devices, equipment
Furniture, doors, walls, etc.

Repeating
Same procedure many times
Many attempts to obtain a difficult result

Repairing
Mechanical devices, equipment
Furniture, doors, walls, etc.

Repeating
Same procedure many times
Many attempts to obtain a difficult result

Persuading

Influencing others to see your point of view
Using influence with others when money is
Involved. Persuading others to help you

Planning

Anticipating future needs of a company or
Organization. Scheduling a sequence of events
Arranging an itinerary for a trip

Politicking

Generating support for one's ideas within an
organization Generating financial support from
another agency or organization

Predicting

Forecasting physical phenomena
Forecasting psychological asocial events
Forecasting the outcomes of contests
Forecasting economic trends

Preparing

Scientific equipment or specimens
Written materials for a presentation

Project Management

Managing projects with colleagues.

Printing

Using mechanical printing equipment
Printing letters

Representing

Representing an employer to the public

Researching

Extracting information from library, archives,
etc. Obtaining information from other people
(surveys)Obtaining information from physical
data

Reviewing

Reassessing effects of a program
Assessing performance of an individual
Evaluating a play, movie, concert, recital, etc.

Rewriting

Technical language into popular form
Revising manuscripts

Selling

Ideas to others personally
Ideas through writing
Products to individuals
Policies to the public

Setting Up

Arranging for a demonstration of some physical
Apparatus. Getting people and things ready for
a show, an exhibit, etc.

Sketching

Picture of things, people,
Diagrams, Charts, other sy

Processing

The orderly flow of electronic data
Introducing an individual to procedures
of an organization Identifying human
interactions taking place in a group
Channeling information through a system

Programming

Electronic computers
Developing and arranging sequence of
events

Promoting

Through written media
On a personal basis, on-to-one
Arranging financial backing

Proposal Writin

For government funding

Protecting

Protecting people from physical harm
Protecting property from people
Building protective devices or equipment
Preventing destructive natural
phenomena

Questioning

Obtaining evidence in legal situations
Asking creative questions in interview
situations

Reading

Read large amounts of material quickly
Read written material with great care
Read numbers of symbols at a great
distance
Read illegible or very small writing

Speaking

Speaking publicly to an audience
Speaking individually to a group
Speaking on electronic media (radio,
TV, tape recorder, etc.)

Supervising

Directly supervising work of others in a
white
collar setting
Overseeing laborers
Being responsible for maintenance
of a physical plant,building, set of
apartments, etc.

Talking

For long periods of time
Able to sustain social chatter

Teaching

In a school or college classroom
Individuals to perform certain tasks
Tutoring individuals in certain subjects

Team Unit Leader

Working with a group
Working with an individual
Helping others be leaders in their field
and the unit be the best in it's functional
area.

Time Management

Organizing time efficiently so that many
tasks are completed in a finite time period
Arranging an event so that it occurs at
precisely the right moment

Tolerance

Ability to accept misbehavior or mistakes
by people for whom you are responsible
Being philosophical about lack of
support for work you are doing and
misunderstanding;
lack of reward or recognition

Recording
Numerical quantitative data
Scientific data, using instruments

Record Keeping
Orderly keeping of numerical data records
Keeping log of sequential information
Creating and maintaining files
Clear and accurate financial records
Record of services rendered

Recruiting/Staffing
Attempting to acquire the services of people for an
organization

Rehabilitating
Helping people to resume use of limbs, etc., after injury Working with patients through non-physical
media such as art, music, dance, etc.

Updating
Keeping a file of information up-to-date
Completing historical record of a person
Acquiring new information on an old topic

Website Design
Helping design a website

Working with Precision
On physical materials
With numerical data
In time and space situation calling for little error

Writing
Copywriting for sales
Creative writing – prose, poetry
Expository writing, essays
Report of memo writing

Translating
Expressing words of one language in words of another
Reducing sophisticated language to simpler terms

Treating
Physical ailments of humans or animals

Trouble shooting
Finding sources of difficulty in human relations
Detecting sources of difficulty in physical apparatus

Step Seven- Execute 4 M's- Monitor, Measure, Modify and Meet Individual and Team Objectives

Times and situations change so you as a team member should monitor and modify objectives that are not achievable. You can set up a measuring device so you can track the reports and teams progress. In the end, you want each report and the unit to be successful but you want them to be challenged.

Step Eight - Develop an *Expert Task Book* and place the names of the people according to their expertise in the book

It is a good idea to start and maintain an *Expert Task Book* with the names of those reports who are experts in performing certain tasks. They will receive recognition and you have a list of good coaches.

Step Nine- Help all those who completed all the tasks successfully identify their next position and prepare for it

The title of a report can remain the same but by adding growth tasks to their position, they can get ready for their next targeted position. . You can then give the report an increase in pay and help them grow on the job being a more valuable employee. The farming out of more tasks to team members can help replace people that leave saving the organization recruiting time and money while retaining good loyal people

Bibliography

i Why Great Managers are so Rare 2012, by Randall Beck and Jim Harter

ii Human Resources Institute of Eckland College, St. Petersburg, Florida, 2016 Study

iii "The Leadership Industry' *Fortune Magazine, February 21, 2009 Issue*

iv Kotter, John. *The Leadership Factor, The Free Press, 2008.*

v *Kotter, John. A Force of Change: How Leadership Differs from Management,* Harvard Business Press, 2009.

vi "Leadership Styles That Make CEOs" Korn Ferry Study in August 10, 2006. *USA Today*

vii *"Superior CEOs" Fortune Magazine, June 21, 2005.*

viii *McCall, John and Lombardo, M.M. "Off the Track: Why and How Successful Executives Get Derailed", June 2003*

ix Maxwell, John, *Developing the Leaders Around You.* Thomas Nelson Publisher, 1995.

x "The Strategic Leadership Analysis Program", Management Research Group, Portland Maine.

xi Welch, Jack, "Putting People First and Strategy Second", *Fortune Magazine* June, 1999.

xii Higgins, Forster. Study of 164 CEOs on Communication, 2006.

xiii Larkin, Sandra. *Communicating Change,* University Press, 2002

About the Author

Dr. Mike Mulligan founded and serves as CEO of Mulligan & Associates, a 30 year career and executive coaching firm. He has counseled and coached over 2,000 CEOs, presidents, senior executives and managers from all industries. Two thirds of those he counseled had been released from their positions by their organization. When he asked them why they were released, many said there was a lack of communication and engagement between them and their boss. They barely talked to each other. The research shows a disengaged boss can let talented people sit on the sidelines and drive them out the door. Dr. Mulligan learned much about leadership and management from the conversations he had with his clients. .

Prior to Mulligan & Associates, Dr. Mulligan served as Management Development Director for Century 21 of Northern Illinois where he directed a staff of six consultants and taught in the Management Development Academy. He and his staff helped 400 franchise owners and their management team plan , hire high performing people and make profit.

Dr. Mulligan has written six books and developed over 15 assessments. He has his Ph.D. in counseling from the University of Georgia and his M.A. in counseling from Michigan State. His doctoral dissertation focused on how to help those entering management excel as team leaders. He worked in high education for 16 years (American College Testing Program, The University of Georgia, Georgia Tech and Michigan State) helping young adults with career and college planning.

Helping Team Members & the Unit Be Best in Field

Unitas

Mirabile

Vinculum

The Wonderful Bond of Unity

Printed in the United States
by Baker & Taylor Publisher Services

Printed in the United States
by Baker & Taylor Publisher Services